TOUR OF THE LAKE DISTRICT

About the Author

Jim Reid lives on the northern fringe of the Lake District. An outdoors enthusiast, he will avoid any office tasks given the slightest opportunity to head for the hills. Educated at Newcastle and Lancaster universities, he has made a living variously and precariously as an ecologist, school teacher, youth hostel warden, restaurateur and landscape gardener. When the writing bug takes over, subjects close to his heart are travel, food, nature and hillwalking.

About the Book

Two years in the making, the *Tour of the Lake District* was written and researched while running a Lakeland youth hostel. All the routes have been carefully chosen and walked, the author muttering into a Dictaphone to ensure descriptions are accurate when written up in the evening. The photographs were taken using an old Leica 35mm camera with Summicron lenses, generally on Velvia film.

TOUR OF THE LAKE DISTRICT

by
Jim Reid

2 POLICE SQUARE, MILNTHORPE, CUMBRIA LA7 7PY
www.cicerone.co.uk

First edition 2007
ISBN 13: 978-1-85284-496-7
© Jim Reid 2007

Acknowledgements

Writing is a solitary task, but impossible without the help and encouragement of a
good many people. First, I must thank my friends and colleagues in the YHA for
their support and hospitality during my ramblings. In particular I wish to thank
Dave Waugh, who first envisaged such a book some years previously, and
unknowingly paved the way for myself when later I came up with the same idea.
I must thank Celine for her extreme patience, proofreading, and all-round support. Thanks to all my hillwalking companions and family over the past two years,
without whose encouragement and feedback the project would have certainly
never come to fruition.

Finally, I must thank that most special of companions, ever silent and stoical
in the face of changeable Lakeland weather – Her Hairiness The Dog. Just don't
get diarrhoea again the next time we have to share a small tent.

Notice to Readers

Readers are advised that while every effort is taken by the author to ensure
the accuracy of this guidebook, changes can occur which may affect the
contents. It is advisable to check locally on transport, accommodation,
shops, etc., but even rights of way can be altered.

The author would welcome information on any updates and changes
sent through the publishers.

Cover photo: Below Great Gable, a crossroads of routes, at the very centre of the
Lake District

CONTENTS

PREFACE

Until I started on this book, I thought I knew the Lake District well. Now I'm not so sure. For all the days I've spent hiking the fells, I'm still discovering paths I'd never previously walked, and places I've never quite got around to visiting. At my desk, working on my book in the winter months, my notepad fills with places I want to *re*visit – when the snow comes, when the bluebells are out, when the red deer are in rut…

And so it may be with you. Perhaps you are a seasoned Lakeland fell walker, perhaps you live here, or maybe you are considering a visit for the first time.

Whichever is the case, there is something in this book for you. If you have a week off work – great – walk the Tour in its entirety. It will take you seven days, and by the end of it you'll be sure to know this amazing place a little better. Got two weeks free? Even better – time enough for a few side trips; the suggestions for short walks in Part 4 should keep you out of mischief. Even if your explorations are just limited to snatched weekends, you can still dip into these pages for inspiration.

Enjoy your time in the hills. In researching this book, I certainly have.

Jim Reid, 2007

Typical Lakeland scenery, from a footpath above Thirlmere

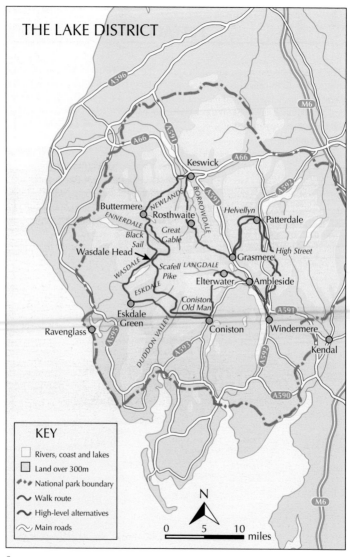

THE LAKE DISTRICT

A596

M6

A66

A591

Keswick

A66

A592

Buttermere

NEWLANDS

BORROWDALE

Helvellyn

Patterdale

ENNERDALE

Rosthwaite

Black
Sail

Great
Gable

High Street

Wasdale Head

Scafell
Pike

LANGDALE

Grasmere

WASDALE

Elterwater

Ambleside

ESKDALE

Coniston
Old Man

A591

Ravenglass

A595

Eskdale
Green

DUDDON VALLEY

A593

Coniston

Windermere

A592

Kendal

A590

A590

M6

KEY

☐ Rivers, coast and lakes

☐ Land over 300m

•◆• National park boundary

∿ Walk route

∿ High-level alternatives

∿ Main roads

N

0   5   10
miles

PART 1
INTRODUCTION

A peaceful June dawn over Elterwater, with the Langdale Pikes behind (Stage 2)

INTRODUCTION

A dipper bathing in the waters of a rain-swollen beck; my path bordered by the cheer of hawthorns in full bloom; and the lush, deep greens of the lake country resuming its summer colours... as I continued on beyond the last of the dry-stone walls to the open fell, past an alpine tarn and up a scramble on the scree-covered flanks of Great Gable, I was greeted on this occasion with a king's view of the land and water below. Such were the highlights of a day on foot in the Lake District that ended high in the mountains by a wood-burning stove in a former shepherd's bothy now a tiny, isolated and charming youth hostel.

The day had taken me along an ancient, well-worn route used by drovers, traders and marauders through history. A picturesque packhorse bridge I crossed over, built without mortar, had stood the test of three centuries of north country winters. I passed farms first settled by Norsemen who saw there a place to stay and make their own. To walk through the Lake District today is to follow in the footsteps of a long line of explorers, visitors and settlers: from the early tribes who first cut the primeval woods and quarried the hard rock of the fells for their axes, to the 18th-century Romantic poets who immortalised the place in verse and paved the way for the modern-day visitor.

This was but one of the days spent researching the Tour of the Lake District, a 93 mile circular walking trek that takes in some of the best of this beautiful area. The routes of past herdsmen and travellers were the inspiration for this modern-day tour, designed to fit into a week's holiday. It is not intended as an endurance test, although there are suggestions for more demanding, high-level routes for those who like to be physically challenged. Rather the Tour passes over easy to moderate terrain, seeking logical pathways between points of interest, history and natural beauty.

THE LAKE DISTRICT LANDSCAPE

To visitors past and present, the attraction of the Lake District is the landscape. The landscape that spoke of opportunity to the early settlers and provided inspiration for the poets today continues to feed the souls of outdoor lovers. It is an old landscape, defined by the geology beneath its surface. The story of this compact collection of lakes and fells began some 600 million years ago when the mud and sediment that were to become the Skiddaw Slates were laid down in the shallow seas that then covered the area. These, the oldest rocks in the region, are the building blocks of the crumbling, scree-flanked fells in the north and west. Later, the centre of the Lake District was subjected to intense volcanic activity creating the rocks and mountains of the Borrowdale Volcanic Group. This ancient volcanic uprising explains why, when you study a map of the Lake District, as Wordsworth himself observed, all the lakes radiate like spokes on a wheel from a point in the middle of the sheet.

With the end of this period of volcanic activity, the area was once more awash in shallow tropical seas, in which the limestones and sandstones of the Lakeland fringes were deposited. Abruptly, a mere one million years ago, the Lake District turned into something more akin to Greenland. The final stage of nature's great contribution to the landscape saw huge glaciers move down the mountains, carving, grinding, smoothing and polishing, to leave the great valleys and isolated tarns we see today. Time passed, the climate returned to more benign temperatures. Pine and birch colonised the mountain slopes; ash, elm and alder trees advanced up the valleys. The Lake District was ready for its first visitor.

Into this landscape, at a point in time merely thousands of years ago, the first human stepped into the Lake District. With this pioneer the second period of landscape change began, for if nature created the backdrop to the Lake District, man provided the detail – the dry-stone walls, the cleared thwaites, the enigmatic stones of Castlerigg stone circle. The Mesolithic tribes of 6000 years ago would have found a virgin territory of tree-clad hills alive with game. These early settlers began the process of deforestation and, in the Neolithic era, began to rear stock on the fells. Little is known of these prehistoric cultures and civilisations, and less is understood. It is known that they traded their precious axes with tribes in Ireland and the Isle of Man – these tools being hewn from the hard, fine-grained volcanic tuffs outcropping in places such as Pike of Stickle in Langdale. They built impressive stone circles requiring teamwork and co-operation. Tantalizing evidence of their settlement in the fells remains in cup- and ring-marked rocks and in post holes that supported long-gone roof timbers.

The Bronze Age, and later Celtic and Roman cultures, brought successively more advanced civilisation to the area. Perhaps the most lasting legacy of the Celts is the name Cumbria itself, derived from *Cymru* ('land of the Welsh'). The arrival of the Romans brings the story into the early historical period, and in the Lake District they left lasting reminders of their settlement (at Ambleside for example) and established major routes through the fells such as High Street, linking the forts at Ambleside and Brougham, and the tortuous route to the coast via Hardknott fort. The Romans planted crops on the now denuded fells and started the first lead

The approach to Black Sail Youth Hostel winds through scenery carved by glaciers (Stage 7)

mining operations, later to become an important part of the rural economy.

By medieval times most of the traditional industries of the Lake District were well established – amongst them coppicing, quarrying and mining. Herdwick sheep, the hardy breed seen on the fells since at least Viking times, were the basis for an increasingly important wool industry. In keeping the upland flora low and preventing woodland regrowth in the lowlands this breed has had a profound influence on the Lakeland landscape. The transport of wool led to the building of packhorse bridges, the earliest of which date from the medieval period.

The late Middle Ages saw a change in the vernacular architecture of the lake country. Increasingly timber was rejected as a building material in favour of more durable slate, as quarried stone became ever more available and affordable.

Stone characterises perhaps the next most important landscape change in the 18th and 19th centuries, the great period of wall building and the enclosure of the open fields. The miles of dry-stone walls were mainly built with the stone to hand, cast aside by the ancient glaciers. The wall building was undertaken by itinerant gangs contracted by landowners who were keen to enclose land for sheep and cash in on the high price of wool during the Napoleonic Wars.

While the dry-stone wallers were completing their mammoth task of enclosing the fells, the first tourists began to arrive. In this the age of the gentleman traveller, continuing political uncertainty in Europe and, in particular, the French Revolution put the continental Grand Tour on hold; instead the pursuit of the picturesque put the Lake District on the itinerary of the travelling classes. Amongst these early visitors was Thomas West, author of the first guidebook to the Lakes (1778). The arrival of the railway brought further waves of visitors, causing the hitherto quiet village of Windermere to mushroom into a tourist resort. By the time he wrote his seminal *Guide to the Lakes* in 1810, Wordsworth was already lamenting a landscape lost to mass tourism.

* * * * * *

But as I sat by the stove in the mountain hut, seven miles from the nearest tarred road, Wordsworth's troubles were far from my mind. Apart from the crackling of the fire and the low buzz of good conversation, the only sound was the occasional bleating of sheep high on the slopes. In the Lake District, solitude is the preserve of the walker, with mile upon mile of routes open to the public. In a week's walking or so it is possible to see something of this unique landscape, using the old drove roads, packhorse routes and mountain passes, and staying in simple accommodation amidst the hills. It provides an escape for a brief while to a timeless world.

This guide describes such a walk.

ABOUT THE TOUR

The Lakes are well known as premier hill walking country. They are also well served by guidebook writers. As I glance along my bookshelf, dog-eared copies of the late Alfred Wainwright's hand-written guides to the Lakeland fells rub spines with Poucher's books, lavishly illustrated with his magnificent black-and-white photographs. These are just two of the more famous names in the genre.

At least three established long-distance walks include the Lake District – Wainwright's Coast to Coast passes through the western fells before heading east to Shap and Yorkshire; the Dales Way concludes at Windermere; and the Cumbria Way bisects the county with a line through the central fells. But there is no definitive, purely *Lake District* long-distance route.

Offering a flavour of each of the main Lakeland valleys, and time to stop and wonder at their charms – a

hidden waterfall in Eskdale, the morning mist over Buttermere, the tour described in this book leads quickly away from the busy tourist centres to the quiet pleasures of the fell country. Designed as a scenic tour of the Lake District, the route is primarily one of valleys and passes, rather than a tick-list of peaks attained. The shepherds and drovers chose their paths well, logical links from one valley to the next, and many of these ancient ways have been chosen for this walk. All footpaths and bridleways used are on established rights of way.

The walk starts at the railway terminus at **Windermere** town, quickly leaving the crowds behind to gain a little height and give a view over the ground to be covered in the next few days. The route continues onwards along a drove road to **Ambleside**, before heading over Loughrigg to the **Langdale valley** and the heart of the Lake District. It then passes through

The descent into Wasdale from Scafell Pike is steep and direct (High Level 2)

the beautifully wooded slate mining areas of **Elterwater** and **Tilberthwaite** to the lakeshore village of **Coniston** under the shadow of the Old Man, one of Lakeland's best-known peaks. From Coniston, another drove road leads over Walna Scar to peaceful **Dunnerdale** before dropping into **Eskdale**.

The route from Eskdale to **Wasdale** is a picturesque, easy day of woods, fields and country pubs. From here, now in the quiet and less visited western fells, the way leads to wild **Ennerdale** and Black Sail Youth Hostel, the most remote point on the walk. Then, it descends through Scarth Gap pass to dramatic views of the **Buttermere valley** and through the lakeside woods to Buttermere village.

A day through the bracken-covered fellsides of **Newlands valley** leads to the market town of **Keswick**, and a welcome dose of civilisation after a few days in the wilds.

South from Keswick, the walk offers picture-postcard views of **Derwentwater** and then continues on through the lush scenery of **Borrowdale** before heading up into the high country to reach **Grasmere**. Leaving Wordsworth's home village, the route then heads over to **Ullswater** before returning back to Windermere via the **Troutbeck valley**.

Planning and preparation

Much of the route uses ancient trails linking the valleys that were established by traders and travellers in times past

STAGE	ROUTE	DISTANCE
Stage 1	Windermere to Ambleside	6½ miles (10.5km)
Stage 2	Ambleside to Elterwater	5 miles (8km)
Stage 3	Elterwater to Coniston	6 miles (9.5km)
Stage 4	Coniston to Eskdale	11 miles (17.5km)
Stage 5	Eskdale to Wasdale	7½ miles (12km)
Stage 6	Wasdale to Black Sail	7 miles (11.5km)
Stage 7	Black Sail to Buttermere	4 miles (6km)
Stage 8	Buttermere to Keswick	9½ miles (15km)
Stage 9	Keswick to Rosthwaite	8 miles (13km)
Stage 10	Rosthwaite to Grasmere	7½ miles (12km)
Stage 11	Grasmere to Patterdale	7¾ miles (12.5km)
Stage 12	Patterdale to Windermere	13 miles (21km)
TOTAL		**92¼ miles (148.5km)**

15

for their relative ease and safety – a drover would not have willingly taken his herd over the high peaks when a suitable alternative through a mountain pass was available. Today these trails make perfect sense for a long-distance walking route – well established yet often quiet; scenic without being overly strenuous; an engaging experience rather than simply a walk between points of interest. The intention of the Tour is to lead the walker into some of the most visually stunning and historically interesting scenery in Britain, and to experience its wildness, nature and people first hand. It is not intended as an endurance test.

Any moderately fit person with some experience of walking could undertake the Tour. A simple fitness check would be to load up a rucksack with the amount of gear you intend to carry (this will vary on whether you plan to camp or stay in hotels). Now check whether you can comfortably and enjoyably walk, say, 10 miles over undulating but not mountainous terrain with such a load. If not, spend some time in the weeks and months leading up to your trip building up your stamina with small walks until you reach this level of fitness.

The main route has been divided into 12 short stages between potential overnight stops (see table p15). In some cases these stopping points may be villages with a wide range of hotels, hostels and B&Bs; in other cases they may be simply a solitary youth hostel up in the fells.

These 12 stages can be combined to create longer days, or you can make your own intinerary based on shorter days. Combining several of the shorter stages could create a seven-day walk, well within the capabilities of the averagely fit walker. In this way the Tour comfortably fits into a week's holiday, with travelling time at either end. (Your itinerary is likely to be based around the availability of accommodation and facilities, which are detailed in the table on p18.)

If you have more than a week, consider timetabling rest days or days to explore the surroundings from one of the overnight halts. You might be able to fit in some of the high-level alternative routes in Part 3 and the day walks in Part 4, if time and energy permit.

High-level alternatives

For those for whom the pull of the high mountains is too great to resist, there are some excellent high-level walking alternatives described in Part 3. These include options for Coniston Old Man, Scafell Pike (England's highest mountain) and Helvellyn.

Each of these high-level alternatives can be substituted for a stage of the main Tour. For example, for the walk between Coniston and Eskdale, you have the choice of the main route Stage 4, following the Walna Scar road, or taking the high-level alternative route 1 (High Level 1) over Coniston Old Man – both end in Eskdale.

The final part of the high-level route to Buttermere is on an easy footpath through lakeshore woods (High Level 3)

FACILITIES ALONG THE ROUTE

	Hotel B&B	Hostel or camping barn	Camping	Pub food	Cafe	Shop for food	Walking supplies	Post office	Telephone box	Bus	Cash machine
Windermere	✓✓✓	✓✓	✗	✓✓✓	✓✓✓	✓✓	✓✓✓	✓	✓✓✓	✓✓	✓✓
Ambleside	✓✓✓	✓✓	✗	✓✓✓	✓✓✓	✓✓	✓✓✓	✓	✓✓✓	✓✓	✓✓
Elterwater	✓✓	✓	✗	✓	✗	✓	✗	✓	✓	✓	✗
Coniston	✓✓✓	✓✓	✓	✓✓✓	✓✓	✓	✓	✓	✓✓	✓	✓
Eskdale	✓✓	✓✓	✓	✓	✗	✓	✗	✓	✓	✗	✗
Wasdale	✓✓	✓	✓	✓✓	✗	✓	✓	✗	✓	✗	✗
Black Sail	✗	✓	✗	✗	✗	✗	✗	✗	✗	✗	✗
Buttermere	✓✓	✓✓	✓	✓✓	✓	✗	✗	✗	✓	✗	✗
Keswick	✓✓✓	✓	✓	✓✓✓	✓✓✓	✓✓	✓✓✓	✓	✓✓✓	✓✓	✓✓✓
Rosthwaite	✓✓✓	✓	✓	✓✓	✓✓	✓	✓	✓	✓	✓	✗
Grasmere	✓✓✓	✓✓	✗	✓✓✓	✓✓✓	✓	✓	✓	✓✓	✓✓	✓
Patterdale	✓	✓	✓	✓✓	✗	✓	✓	✓	✓	✓	✗

Key ✓ = one or very few – for buses, this may mean a seasonal or infrequent service
✓✓ = more than one – at least hourly service in case of buses
✓✓✓ = numerous
✗ = none or no information available. For campsites this may mean there is no official campsite, but opportunities for wild camping may exist – or may mean the nearest campsite is more than two miles away.
Note: It may seem odd in the age of mobile phones to indicate where telephone boxes are to be found, yet outside the main tourist towns mobile phone reception is sporadic, and especially patchy in the valleys, where our route takes us.

HIGH LEVEL TOUR: A suggested itinerary for an eight-day trek			
Day 1	Stage 1	Windermere to Ambleside	6½ miles (10.5km)
	Stage 2	Ambleside to Elterwater	5 miles (8km)
	Stage 3	Elterwater to Coniston	6 miles (9.5km)
Day 2	High Level 1	Coniston to Eskdale via the Old Man and Hardknott	11 miles (17.5km)
Day 3	High Level 2	Eskdale to Wasdale Head via Scafell Pike	10 miles (16.5km)
Day 4	High Level 3	Wasdale Head to Buttermere via Great Gable	9¾ miles (15.5km)
Day 5	Stage 8	Buttermere to Keswick	9½ miles (15km)
Day 6	Stage 9	Keswick to Rosthwaite	8 miles (13km)
	Stage 10	Rosthwaite to Grasmere	7½ miles (12km)
Day 7	High Level 4	Grasmere to Patterdale via Helvellyn	10 miles (16km)
Day 8	High Level 5	Patterdale to Windermere via High Street	14 miles (23km)
TOTAL			**97¼ miles (156.5km)**

If your fitness and experience levels are up to it, it's well worth considering at least one of these high-level alternatives – on a fine day your efforts will certainly be rewarded with an experience to remember. Note the 'fine day' caveat – conversely there is no joy in climbing a Lakeland peak in the mist, to arrive at the summit tired and cold with a view of – mist! (It is particularly important to read the sections on 'Navigation and Outdoor Safety' in this Introduction if you are taking the high-level routes.)

Taking all the high-level alternatives in the guide would create a challenging eight-day walk of just over 97 miles (156.5km).

High-level Tour
The box above shows a suggested itinerary for an eight-day trek, taking in all the high-level options.

WHEN TO GO

Undeniably the busiest times in the Lake District are the school holidays, especially July and August, but also the Easter week, the days surrounding New Year and the two 'half term' weeks usually late February and late October. If possible avoid planning your trip for these times, as accommodation is stretched and priced at a premium.

Aside from people, the other deciding factor on when to go is the weather. Throughout the year, the weather in the Lake District is famed for its changeability; an early morning downpour can give way to a sunny afternoon and vice versa. However, clear skies and fine walking weather *can* be found at any time of the year, but between November and March these days are precious and usually accompanied by frosty mornings and icy conditions on the fells. Walking in the autumn and winter months is also hampered by shorter day length, and from November 1st there is a feeling that business has closed for the winter – both transport and accommodation can be a problem. This said, a well-planned and pre-booked late autumn tour could be rewarded with empty trails and vivid colours, if the weather is stable. A winter tour on the other hand is reserved for the very determined, experienced and well-equipped walker.

Spring arrives a little later in the Lakes than most parts of England, but by May the frosts have usually gone from the valleys, and the greening and flowering of the lake country can be enjoyed in relative solitude, with

LAKE DISTRICT EVENTS CALENDAR		
March	Daffodil and Spring Flower Show	Ambleside
May	Jazz Festival	Keswick
June	Beer Festival	Keswick
	Country Fair	Ullswater
	Rushbearing Festival	Ambleside
July	Ambleside Sports	Ambleside
	Country Fair	Coniston
August	Lake District Summer Music Festival	Various
	Grasmere Sports	Grasmere
	Agricultural Show	Keswick
September	Shepherd's Meet	Borrowdale
	Eskdale Show	Eskdale
October	Wasdale Show	Wasdale
	Buttermere Show	Buttermere
November	Words by the Water Literature Festival	Keswick
	Kendal Mountain Festival	Kendal
	Biggest Liar Competition	Wasdale
December	Victorian Fair	Keswick

Wastwater as seen from Great Gable summit – of all the high fells, Great Gable is closest to the centre of the Lakes (High Level 3)

accommodation more easy to find than in the summer. Moving towards peak season, the months of June and early July can see some warm weather, and offer long, light days. Even in the summer months the Tour will take you through peaceful, less frequented valleys and woodlands – but be prepared for crowds in the 'honey pot' centres of Ambleside and Keswick.

The Lake District is a living community that holds various events throughout the year, and you may wish to time your visit to coincide with one of these. Particularly good for local colour are the many agricultural shows, which are held mainly in the summer months and often feature sheep dog trials and traditional sports such as Cumberland wrestling. The box on p20 lists some of the main events of the Lakeland year, and more details can be found from Tourist Information Centres – see Appendix 1 for contact details.

WEATHER FACTS

There is no denying the fact that the Lake District sees a lot of rain – but some areas within the National Park attract more than their fair share. Seathwaite, just off the Tour's main route, has the dubious honour of being the wettest inhabited place in the British Isles. In an average year it can expect 3300mm of rain. This is over twice as much as Keswick, a mere seven miles away, which gets only 1470mm! Head further to the east beyond the high fells to the town of Penrith, and you'll find a comparatively arid climate – only 870mm per annum, less than a third of Seathwaite's rainfall.

ACCOMMODATION

To book ahead or leave it to chance? The romantic image of the hiker out on the trail deciding on a whim where to rest their weary feet for the night is an appealing one, but today's high-season hiker may be in for an unpleasant shock when confronted with a row of uninviting 'no vacancy' signs. The decision to book ahead for accommodation is ultimately a personal one, but some points for consideration are included here.

The backpacker carrying a tent and cooking equipment is best able to keep a flexible itinerary (see 'Camping and Camping Barns' for further information), but clearly at a cost in weight carried. Particularly on the high-level routes, carrying the extra weight of **camping** equipment can seriously detract from the enjoyment of a walk.

However, it allows flexibility, as decisions on where to stay can be made on the spot. If there is no official campsite at day's end, a word with a farmer can often secure a pitch; or, further from habitation, discreet wild camping may be an option, though you have no legal right to do so.

Those intending to stay in **hostels** during high season, or even at the shoulder times of late spring and early autumn, may see the larger hostels booked out to school groups, leaving the solo traveller without a bed. A phone call, even a day or two in advance, will prevent an unwelcome surprise.

As regards **B&Bs** and **hotels**, apart from exceptionally busy periods, the larger centres of Windermere, Ambleside and Keswick will always have some beds available

A bird's-eye view of Buttermere from Red Pike (Stage 7)

The Sun Inn at Coniston, passed on the way to
Church Beck and the Old Man (High Level 1)

Wastwater, the deepest of the Lakes next to Lakeland's tallest summits

somewhere, although a degree of phoning around and leg work may be needed to find accommodation of the type and price range you require. Tourist Information offices in the larger villages and towns usually have details of current availability.

Several stages of the Tour end in smaller villages, where there are very few accommodation options available. In these cases contact details of individual establishments are included in the route description – clearly, booking ahead is strongly advised to prevent lengthy and costly end-of-day taxi rides to civilisation.

Camping and camping barns

At the budget end of the scale, camping offers the most flexibility. Most of the official campsites on the main route of the Tour are small, basic establishments operated by farmers or the National Trust, typically charging £5–7 per night for a pitch. Expect running water and toilet facilities for this; some also have hot showers and a small shop.

Wild camping is also possible in some places along the route. If close to habitation, you must always ask for permission before making camp. Beyond the outlying boundary walls of the Lakeland valleys, on the open fell, wild camping is unofficially tolerated – but there is no legal right to camp. Again use sensitivity and discretion.

Camping barns (also described as stone tents) and bunkhouses are increasingly popular. Sitting roughly

between camping and hostelling in terms of comfort levels, these are usually old farm outbuildings given a new lease of life as simple accommodation for the hiking market. Charging around £6 per night they offer basic facilities, usually mattresses on sleeping platforms (bring your own sleeping bag and cooking gear), toilets, and sometimes a shower and wood-burning stove. Dogs may be permitted – check before arrival. There are camping barns at Buttermere on the main route and at Gillerthwaite – three miles off the route, in Ennerdale.

Youth hostels

These have come a long way since their inception in the 1930s. Gone are the days of 'chores' and large dormitories. The word 'youth' is also misleading; they are open to – and used by – all age groups. On the main route of the Tour there are three independent hostels at Grasmere, Windermere and Ambleside, and several belonging to the YHA network. In all the YHA hostels en route you can expect good quality, reasonably priced food as well as a bed for the night. Twin and family rooms, occasionally en suite, may also be available. As a general rule, expect to pay £12–16 per night to stay at a youth hostel, which may include breakfast.

B&Bs and hotels

These vary enormously in style and price. The more modest bed and breakfast establishments start at around £18 per person per night for two sharing a room, off-season, in say Ambleside or Windermere, but can easily run to £30+ per night at peak times or in a particularly popular location. For this, expect a sink, coffee-making facilities and a TV in the room. Most rooms in B&Bs now have en-suite facilities, but not all.

For a mid-range hotel or room in a country pub, expect to pay £40–60 per person per night.

Many B&Bs and hotels will insist on a minimum stay of two nights, especially at weekends – less than helpful for a walking tour. Check with individual establishments.

FOOD AND SUPPLIES

Compared with national parks in other parts of the world, food and supplies pose much less of a problem to a walker in the Lake District – rarely are you more than a few miles from a cafe, pub or shop, so there is no need to carry a week's worth of supplies.

If staying in a hotel, B&B or youth hostel, breakfast is usually included or available – and in this part of the world, hearty. The 'full English' is *de rigueur*; fear not, the calories will be burnt off during the day! Most establishments will offer a lighter alternative of cereals, yoghurt or croissants. You may be able to order a packed lunch to take with you for your day in the hills – accommodation providers

in the Lakes are well used to catering to the needs of walkers.

Campers are more likely to need to stock up on provisions. At the start of the walk in Windermere there is large Booths supermarket right next door to the railway station; in Ambleside a small Co-op on Compston Road; and in Keswick the large Lakes Foodstore by the bus station. In the smaller villages, basic provisions can be found in the post office / general store where these exist – see facilities chart above. Many of the outdoor gear shops in the area stock dehydrated food for the ultra-light-weight backpacker, but more economic alternatives can be had from the supermarkets.

As regards eating out, as you might expect the largest choice is again in Ambleside, Grasmere, Keswick and Windermere, where you will find everything from bakeries and sandwich bars to hiker's cafes and bistro restaurants. A do-it-yourself lunch from a supermarket or bakery can be had for £2–3, or a modest sit-down snack in a cafe for £5.

Evening dining in the Lake District, both in the towns and in the villages, is dominated by the pubs and hotels. The overall quality of bar food has improved greatly in recent years, with healthy, home-cooked options often available. Local specialities such as Cumberland sausage, Borrowdale trout and the ubiquitous sticky toffee pudding share menu space with more eclectic offerings. Food in the pubs is usually generously portioned. Price varies with the location and aspirations of the chef, but a spend of £8–11 should usually secure a filling main course bar meal.

Vegetarians are well catered for in the Lake District, with an unusually high concentration of dedicated restaurants and cafes, and vegetarian options available at most food outlets. Dedicated vegetarian cafes include Zefferellis in Ambleside, the Rowan Tree in Grasmere and the Lakeland Pedlar in Keswick.

Other supplies such as outdoor equipment, maps and pharmaceutical supplies are easily obtained in the towns, and even the smallest village shop will usually stock the local Ordnance Survey map, toothbrush or roll of 35mm print film should you run low.

When you are in the towns of Windermere, Ambleside and Keswick, remember to stock up on that most basic of commodities – cash. Between Coniston and Keswick you will not encounter a cash machine or bank on the Tour!

Trains

The start (and end point) of the Tour is Windermere railway station. Windermere is the terminus of the branch line from Oxenholme, which is in turn a stop on the main Virgin Trains west coast service from London. Journey time to Windermere from London, changing at Oxenholme, is approx 4hrs, with 3–4 services per day. There is also a direct

Boats, Derwentwater (Stage 8)

service from Manchester Airport to Windermere – journey time 2¼ hours, with 3 services per day.

Buses

The central Lakes is the area best served by buses, with route 555 plying between Windermere, Ambleside, Grasmere and Keswick year round and a bus every hour or so. From Ambleside, the Langdale Rambler (route 516) serves Elterwater; buses are daily but infrequent. Also from Ambleside, the 505 Coniston Rambler service links the town to Coniston village; again services are daily but infrequent.

From Keswick, the Borrowdale Rambler (79) follows perhaps the most picturesque of Lakeland bus routes, and provides a useful year-round hourly service. Between April and October the Honister Rambler

Elderflowers in bloom, late summer

links Buttermere with Keswick (service almost hourly).

Patterdale is less well served by public transport, and for much of the year is accessible from the Penrith direction only by the infrequent 108 service. However, from the end of July to the end of August there is also the 517 Kirkstone Rambler service (infrequent) between Windermere and Patterdale village. This service continues, weekends only, to the end of October.

The western lakes – Eskdale, Ennerdale and Wasdale – are not connected by regular public transport. Eskdale does have the wonderful 'Ratty' narrow-gauge railway, but this is perhaps better enjoyed as a trip in its own right (see the Eskdale section) rather than a means of accessing this part of the Tour!

If planning to walk the Tour as a series of day walks using the bus network, it will usually be worth investing in either a day- or week-long bus pass. Currently a day pass, valid for all buses in the Lakes, costs £8.50.

Cars

The ideal for those walking the Tour would be to come to the Lake District for a week, leaving the car behind. However, if you are unable to set aside a week or more, completing the tour as a series of day walks is a viable option, made all the more easy by using a car. This can be organised either by parking at the beginning of a day's walk and returning by bus at the end, or by using two cars and 'leap frogging'. In either case, make an early start – popular parking areas become very busy by mid-morning in summer. There are fee-charging National Park car parks at Buttermere, Ullswater and Grasmere, and National Trust car parks in Buttermere, Rosthwaite, Wasdale Head and Elterwater. Members of the National Trust can park for free at these four car parks. In addition to these and other district council fee-charging car parks in the towns and villages, there are small car parks dotted about the countryside, usually free. It may also be possible to park discreetly by the roadside for many stages of the Tour. Note that there is no car access (or public transport) to Black Sail. Nearest parking for Black Sail is at Bowness Knott forestry car park by Ennerdale lake or at Gatesgarth in the Buttermere valley.

MONEY AND COSTS

Camping

If you are planning to mix stays in the smaller official campsites with occasional nights wild camping, cooking for yourself along the way, you could spend as little as £10–15 per day on the Tour. The odd meal (or pint) at a wayside pub could up the daily spend to closer to £20.

Hostelling, B&Bs and hotels

Self catering at youth hostels, with the occasional meal out, but with simple do-it-yourself lunches could be enjoyed on a budget of £20–25 per day. Taking all the meal options at a youth hostel could raise the daily spend to around £30. Staying in B&Bs each night and eating out at a pub each evening would require a budget of £40–50 per day. Stay at the more luxurious of Lakeland hotels and the sky's the limit!

Carrying money

It is necessary to carry a certain amount of cash on the Tour. There are ATM cash machines in the streets of Windermere, Ambleside and Keswick only. Some post offices, petrol stations and pubs now have ATMs or may offer 'cash back' on debit cards. A cheque book may be useful for payment at B&Bs, which may not accept credit cards.

WHAT TO TAKE

How much to take?

The short answer is 'as little as possible' provided you take sufficient to complete your journey comfortably and safely. Carrying too much weight will inevitably spoil your enjoyment of the walk.

Essentials

To carry your kit you will need a rucksack. If you are walking the Tour as a series of day hikes, a rucksack with a capacity of 20 litres or so will be sufficient. If you are staying in hostels or

B&Bs, 40 litres will be about right, and if carrying camping equipment 60 litres. Don't be tempted to take a larger rucksack than you need. When you pack it will fill as if by magic with a multitude of heavy objects you do not actually need – only to be jettisoned en route!

For spring to autumn walking, lightweight leather or fabric boots will be sufficient. They will need to be waterproof; look for boots lined with a Goretex or similar membrane for an additional layer of protection. In general lighter boots, and especially the non-leather versions, need less 'breaking in', but be sure to wear new boots on a few training walks to iron out any problems.

A good set of waterproofs are a must for hiking in the Lake District, starting with a waterproof jacket with a hood, and either waterproof trousers or, as some prefer, gaiters. Gaiters are ideal for walking through wet grass and bracken, and worn with shorts they make a comfortable alternative to waterproof trousers in the summer.

What else to take with you is ultimately a personal decision, influenced by what you are prepared to carry and the degree of comfort you like to travel in, but the suggested list below should be a good starting point for planning what to pack in that rucksack.

Suggested equipment list
- Rucksack
- Waterproof liner for rucksack
- Carrier bags for rubbish or keeping things dry
- Walking boots and socks
- Waterproofs
- Base layer – T-shirts or similar, light long-sleeved top

Lilies on Loughrigg Tarn on a calm summer's day (Stage 2)

- Mid-layer – fleece pullover or jacket
- Shorts
- Walking trousers
- Underwear
- Change of clothing for evenings
- Sun hat (summer)
- Warm hat and gloves (spring and autumn)
- Toiletries
- Medication
- Sunscreen and insect repellent
- Toilet paper
- Small first aid kit, with aspirin or similar, and Moleskin or similar for treating blisters
- Torch
- Whistle
- Food
- Water bottle
- Camera and film/memory card
- Maps and compass
- Sunglasses
- Money and cheque book

For camping:
- Tent
- Sleeping bag
- Sleeping mat
- Stove
- Fuel
- Pans and lid
- Pan grab
- Cutlery and pen knife
- Pan scrub
- Mug

NAVIGATION AND OUTDOOR SAFETY

Maps and wayfinding

The Ordnance Survey extracts in this guidebook show the route of the Tour, but inevitably cannot cover much more than 100m or so either side – not much use if by intention or accident you go off exploring the surroundings! To put the walk in context, it is recommended you carry also the four 1:25,000 OS Outdoor Leisure sheets that cover the Lake District, in a waterproof map case, along with a Silva or similar compass. The four OS maps you need are:
- OL4
- OL5
- OL6
- OL7.

Do make sure you can use the compass at least for basic navigational tasks – orientating the map and taking compass bearings. You may not need to use this knowledge on the Tour, but it may give you some reassurance should the cloud descend on a more exposed section.

The 1:25,000 scale 'Superwalker' series by Harvey Maps includes five maps covering the Lake District, and offers an alternative to the Ordnance Survey sheets. You will need all five maps for the Tour:
- South East
- Central
- South West
- West
- East.

Signpost near Deepdale bridge – footpaths and bridleways in the national park are generally well marked

These durable, water-resistant maps are less than half the bulk of the laminated OS equivalents; some walkers also prefer Harvey maps for their clear colour shading, making relief features more obvious – the choice is yours. Recently, Harvey and the BMC have brought out a 1:40,000 Mountain Map of the Lakes – the best map currently available to cover the entire national park in a single sheet. The Mountain Map is a viable alternative to carrying the four separate OS sheets (or five Superwalker maps) and includes useful 1:20,000 enlargements of some mountain summits such as Scafell and Great Gable.

More accessible information on mountain navigation is available in *Map and Compass* by Pete Hawkins (Cicerone Press), www.cicerone.co.uk.

Weather forecasts

In the morning, before finalising your walking plans for the day, it is well worth phoning the Lake District Weatherline on (0870) 550 575. Provided by the Lake District National Park Authority, it provides a weather service tailored to Lakeland hillwalking. Allow a forecast of high winds or low cloud, for example, to influence a decision on whether to attempt a high-level variant or stick to the main route.

On the trail

Both good and poor weather pose potential hazards to walkers in the Lakes. Even in apparently cloudy summer weather, be aware of sunburn and dehydration. Take a sun hat and carry at least two litres of water with you. Remember to apply sun screen to all exposed skin, and don't forget lip protection. Ensure your companions drink a lot of water, and if any show signs of heat exhaustion – stop, get water into them, cool them down as best you can and get help. Indicators that all is not well include giddiness, stumbling, raised body temperature and a rapid pulse.

Hypothermia can be a danger in the Lake District in poorer weather, where wind and rain conspire to lower the body temperature of the victim. However this is much less likely to strike a well-clad and -fed walker. Again, keep an eye on companions to ensure everyone is drinking and eating enough, and watch out for unusual behaviour – irritability, aggression, slurring of speech. If the early stages of hypothermia are suspected, find or improvise shelter as soon as possible with the aim of restoring body warmth, and get help if symptoms do not improve rapidly.

River crossings
Some routes (for example the high-level route over Coniston Old Man, in Dunnerdale) include a river crossing by stepping stones. In others (for example the high-level route in Upper Eskdale) the path crosses a normally shallow beck. In either situation, there may be times when high, fast-moving water makes this unsafe. Be prepared to abandon a river crossing rather than risk life and limb – whether the solution is a brief detour to a bridge or a more lengthy diversion on tarmac roads.

Solo walking
Clearly the solo walker is at a greater risk should something go wrong. You may wish to consider a route-card system, at least on the more remote sections of the Tour. Before setting out, leave route details with a friend, agree a phoning-in time later in the day, and agree a procedure should you not report in on time. All three elements have to be in place for a route-card system to work.

In an emergency
It is important that you are properly equipped (see 'What to Take') for your Tour, and that you are competent in using a map and compass. This will reduce the risk to yourself and your party, and ensure that you can deal with minor accidents and navigational problems. **For emergencies only**, contact the emergency services, including mountain rescue, by dialling 999 from a mobile phone or call box if available.

You cannot ask for mountain rescue directly, but based on the information you give to the switchboard operator, the appropriate response team will be sent out – either by land or by air. Giving precise details of your location and nature of the incident will speed assistance.

If you are on your own or are unable to get to a telephone, summon help with a whistle (or torch if dark). The internationally understood signal is six whistle blasts or torch flashes spread over 1 minute, followed by a minute's pause. Repeat this until an answer is received. This will be three signals per minute followed by a minute's pause.

HABITATS AND WILDLIFE IN THE LAKE DISTRICT

This brief overview describes some of the habitats found in the Lake District, and what you can expect to see while out walking.

Woodlands

Of all England's national parks the Lake District is the most forested, with 270km^2 of woodlands and plantations. Much of the Tour passes through the broad-leaved woodlands of Lakeland's rich green valleys when not passing over the fells. Along with most of England prior to man's arrival on the land, the Lakeland fells would originally have been covered with a blanket of trees, their spread restricted only by altitude or thin soils. Seven thousand years ago, great swathes of oak and elm would have grown up to a treeline at around 700m.

Pollen analysis suggests that the effect of the early prehistoric pasturalists was to massively reduce the number of elm – today very much a minority species, even without Dutch Elm disease. In addition to changing the species mix of the forests, over millennia man completely cleared the original wild wood of the high fells. The soil, left open to the elements, lost its fertility, and with it the ability to support a woodland ecosystem – as a result, the present-day treeline is reduced to around 250–350m. In fact, all the woods in the Lake District today are secondary forest, the original wild wood long since having cleared. However, at Birkrigg and Keskadale in Newlands there are small pockets of forest thought to be descended from the original higher altitude wild wood.

In the valleys today, oak still dominates the woodland scene. The most common woodland type, the sessile oak forests, is found on acidic soils – these woods may also include birch, hazel and holly. On the limestone outcrops, ash woodland dominates, but in the Lakes ash is most commonly found in association with oak. Testimony to the tree's presence is found in placenames such as Ash Landing and Ashness Bridge. Patches of beech woodland are dotted around the Lakes, adding a notable splash of colour to autumn walks.

The mix of tree species in the woodlands today, particularly in the Windermere and Coniston areas, is very much a product of the 17th–19th centuries, when the woods were actively planted and managed for the coppice industry. Hence species such as hazel, oak, ash and birch – all suited to coppicing – are still commonly found together. You may see holly amidst the oak–ash woodlands growing to a considerable size. The broadleaf woodlands harbour creatures such as badgers, foxes and stoats, as well as owls and buzzards.

Beckside woodlands leading from Buttermere towards the Newlands valley (Stage 8)

The 20th century saw some efforts by the Forestry Commission to recolonise the uplands, albeit with larch and spruce. In the specialised habitat of the coniferous plantations you may see seed-loving siskins, with peregrines, sparrowhawks and red squirrels also spotted from time to time. Deer abound, though you are as likely to see roe deer in the shrubbery of Windermere Youth Hostel as in the wilds of Ennerdale forest. Red deer, less common, are also seen in pockets of the Lake District such as Martindale near Ullswater.

On the ground, woodlands host a variety of plants, lichen and fungi. Depending on the time of your visit bluebells, primroses or wood anemone may all be found. Mushroom hunters may find some treasures in the woods – including easily identifiable edibles such as ceps, chanterelles and wood hedgehog.

Hay meadows and grasslands

A vanishing habitat, here as elsewhere in the north of England, traditionally managed meadows now account for only 5km^2 of the Lake District National Park. Those that remain are rich in wild flowers and are regarded as ecologically important. The diversity of plant species in this habitat is due to late cutting times (allowing plants to set seed) and to the less fertile, unimproved soils. (It may seem strange that the very lack of fertility in these fields encourages a great diversity of species. This is because the nutrient-hungry grasses

Robin on a wall at Belle Grange by the shore of Windermere (Short Walk 1)

A summer scene: haymaking in the Newlands valley (Stage 8)

that are found in modern fields, and which are prone to driving out weaker species, cannot thrive in these nutrient-poor conditions.) Here in the old meadows, species such as wood cranesbill, Devil's bit scabious, yellow rattle and varieties of orchid and saxifrage co-exist, long lost in neighbouring fields improved with fertilisers. Yellow wagtails, curlew, skylarks and brown hare also find a home here. If these hay meadows are a rare sight these days, thankfully the verges of out-of-the-way lanes also display some of their characteristics and diversity, with similar species adding a dash of colour in the spring. Particularly in May and June, try to find room in the rucksack for a wild flower guide.

The fellsides

In addition to its lengthy sections through Lakeland woodlands, the Tour crosses many miles between the present day treeline and the high fells – Herdwick country. In this rough grazing land, the fescue and bent grasses battle for ground with the ever-advancing bracken. Periodically, becks and ghylls cut across the fell-side footpaths, providing a habitat for small mountain birds such as ring ouzels, wheatears and whinchats. Very occasionally in the summer months you may encounter an adder basking in the sunshine.

By the wayside you will certainly find hardy hawthorns and hollies taking their chances, and the evergreen shrub juniper, the latter often spotted

Lakeland lambs

in clefts of rock up to around 350m. Above the juniper, you may come across areas of heather and bilberries.

The uplands

The upland areas of the Lakes include a whole range of different habitats. You will certainly have to deal with blanket mire on the Tour, and if your patience holds out you might appreciate the sphagnum mosses, insectivorous sundew plants, bog asphodel and cotton grass to be found in these boggy conditions. The highest upland areas of the Lakes also host alpine habitats amidst the thin rocky soils,

with plants sometimes found at much lower altitudes than their European cousins. Although the limestone outcrops of the south of the county may be richer in plant diversity, even the Helvellyn area, for example – at first sight a barren rocky outcrop – conceals plants such as dwarf willows, alpine saxifrage and alpine meadow rue. The Lake District is also home to England's only true montane butterfly species, the mountain ringlet, found only on land over 350m.

The crags are home to several species of birds of prey. Buzzards and raven are common in the Lake

District, and peregrine numbers are now healthy also. Unfortunately, Haweswater no longer has a nesting pair of golden eagles, a loss not just for the Lakes, but England as a whole. Ospreys on the other hand are faring better, and can be viewed from the observation areas set up around Bassenthwaite.

Lakes and rivers

The lakes of the area support several species of fish, some of them rare, such as the arctic char, a relic from the Ice Age that survives in the nutrient-poor waters of Ennerdale lake, while the ubiquitous trout finds its way onto many a Lake District menu. Common sights on the lakes are nesting ducks, grebes and cormorants, as well as geese when in migration. On the rivers and becks, look out for birds such as the dipper, wagtail and kingfisher. There have been reports of otters in Lakeland rivers again in recent years.

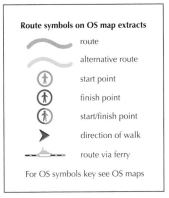

Route symbols on OS map extracts

route
alternative route
start point
finish point
start/finish point
direction of walk
route via ferry

For OS symbols key see OS maps

HOW TO USE THIS GUIDE

The Tour is described in twelve stages (Part 2), and includes many points of interest along the route. In the main route description (and in Parts Three and Four) the guide includes sections from the 1:50,000 OS Landranger maps on which the route is highlighted (for a key to the additional symbols used on the maps, see below), and there are also useful profiles that show the height gain and loss throughout the day. The main places and landmarks along the route are highlighted in **bold** in the text to help with route finding.

The **high-level alternatives** that can be taken on particular sections of the route are described in Part Three. Part Four gives nine **short walks** that can be taken from a number of the overnight stops, should you wish to linger rather than to dash off immediately next morning on the Tour.

At the beginning of the route description for each stage is a box giving details of distances, times, ascent, maps, start point, accommodation and refreshments. **Distances** for each stage are given in miles and kilometres; shorter lengths are described within the text in metres – think 'yards' if your brain is still programmed with imperial units!

Times given are a rough approximation only. For the high-level routes a time range is given – the fit and unloaded may think in terms of the faster time; for the heavily loaded or easily fatigued the longer time may be more realistic.

The guide is to be used in conjunction with the recommended Ordnance Survey or Harveys **maps**, and these are listed in the box.

Places en route offering **accommodation** and **refreshments** appear in the box at the start of each stage, and at the appropriate place in the route

description. At the end of a number of routes is a box for 'Further exploration', which indicates which **short walk** in Part Four can be done from the overnight stop. Further details, together with information about **transport**, are given at the end of each stage in the 'Facilities' box; these are without either positive or negative recommendation. Contact details and availability do change, but are correct at time of going to press.

GLOSSARY AND ABBREVIATIONS

Beck, ghyll	stream / watercourse
Dog-leg	a short sideways shift in the path: eg. 'dog-leg right'
Fell	hill or hillside (northern England)
Finger post	official wooden signpost showing rights of way
Hairpin	very sharp turn in the path, almost doubling back
Ladder-stile	wooden stile over wall
LDNP	Lake District National Park
Lonnin	lane, used here specifically to describe one bordered by walls
NT	National Trust
Squeeze stile	narrow crafted gap in dry-stone wall
Trig. point	concrete column on hill tops used by map makers for triangulation

Patterdale and meadow in June, with the flowers at their peak (Stage 12)

PART 2
THE TOUR

STAGE 1
Windermere to Ambleside

Distance	6½ miles (10.5km)
Time	2¾hrs
Total ascent	360m (1190ft)
Maps	OS 1:25,000 OL7, Harvey Superwalker South East and Central sheets
Start point	Windermere railway station, SD414986
Accommodation	Windermere, Troutbeck, Ambleside
Refreshments	Windermere, Troutbeck, Ambleside

The Tour begins and ends at Windermere railway station. Stage 1 is a gentle intro-duction to the Lakeland fells. The six miles over undemanding terrain are easily accomplished in a summer's afternoon to allow those arriving on a midday train to get underway on their first day. Alternatively, if you are staying overnight at Windermere Youth Hostel – or if a morning start is possible – the stage can be combined with Stage 2 for a leisurely day's stroll to Elterwater, allowing time to indulge oneself in the coffee shops of Ambleside halfway through the walk and still arrive in Elterwater by mid-afternoon.

There is little climbing today, aside from a short pull from the Windermere Hotel up to the viewpoint on Orrest Head. Instead, it is a day of mainly level walking following ancient byways lined with wayside flowers, of tumbling water-falls, broadleaf woodlands and glimpses between the trees of the route over the days to come.

The railway terminus at the town of Windermere is a natural starting point for any tour of the Lakes, and has been since Wordsworth's day. Prior to 1847, what is now Windermere town was merely a small village called Nibthwaite, but the arrival of the railway changed all that, opening up the Cumbrian towns and fells for all to enjoy. Wordsworth, despite having written his popular *Guide to the Lakes* – arguably the most influential guidebook to the Lakes ever written – recoiled in horror at the thought of the masses descending by train to spoil his beloved Lake District. When the proposals for the Lake District line were first put forward in 1844, Wordsworth was a most vociferous opponent. Largely due to the campaigning efforts of the poet and his allies, the railway was halted at

Windermere, rather than pushing on to Ambleside or, heaven forbid, Grasmere – one can imagine Wordsworth penning irate letters to the *Morning Post* and the prime minister at the thought of the lower classes spoiling the views from his home at Rydal Mount!

From the **railway station** cross the main road to the Windermere Hotel, picking up a footpath to Orrest Head indicated by a big white sign by the hotel's driveway. The tarred driveway zigzags up hill past Elleray Wood Lodge (a blacksmith's workshop), and turns into an inviting track through woodland. As the track runs into the woodland, keep right and head sharply uphill through the beech trees for about 100m to the top of the little woodland. On meeting a dry-stone wall here turn right, and follow the well-worn path up to the top **of Orrest Head** viewpoint. ▶

Leave the viewpoint by the footpath leading down to the tarred lane at the other side of Orrest Head near a farm with a prominent white building. Reach the lane via a stone stile next to a metal field gate, then turn left and walk downhill for 600m past the white farm to a row of three handsome stone buildings – **Crosses Farm**. Take

From here you can gaze out over the lake – pick out Belle Isle, the largest of the islands, Coniston Old Man over to the east, and further north the Langdale Pikes.

From Orrest Head, enjoy views over Windermere to Claife Heights and the Furness fells

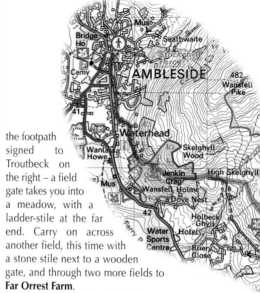

the footpath signed to Troutbeck on the right – a field gate takes you into a meadow, with a ladder-stile at the far end. Carry on across another field, this time with a stone stile next to a wooden gate, and through two more fields to **Far Orrest Farm**.

As you weave through the farm you are faced with a batch of signs at the far side – take the footpath signed to Troutbeck along a track to the left. When this access track reaches a lane go straight across onto a public footpath to reach the Windermere to Kirkstone Pass road.

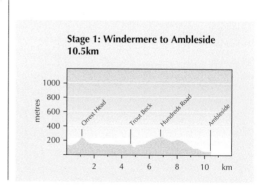

Stage 1: Windermere to Ambleside 10.5km

Turn right and follow this busier road uphill for 300m before picking up a bridleway by a bus stop on the left, to Town End. The bridleway takes you first into a leafy ravine, pungent with wild garlic in season, where the waters of Trout Beck slice through the valley floor. Two footbridges at a brief climb bring you out at the first houses of the hamlet **of Town End**. ▶

From these first houses, turn right up Bridge Lane to the National Trust property of Townend (open afternoons Easter to October), and bear right again to reach the centre of the village by the post office. Before hurrying past it's worth taking the time to visit Townend, a prime example of a 17th-century yeoman farmer's cottage, which arguably offers a greater insight to this period of Lakeland life than the more visited former home of Wordsworth in Grasmere. ▶

Accommodation:
for Windermere YH (700m) turn left here down Bridge Lane.

Refreshments:
The post office is open six days a week in summer for basic provisions and take-away teas, coffees and ice creams that you can enjoy on the bench under the cherry tree.

From the post office, pick up the bridleway indicated by a finger post 'Robin Lane' which climbs gently away from the village. At last you're off the tarmac again and onto a well-maintained track, with views back over the Troutbeck valley. After 700m ignore the track to the left, and keep to the main track indicated by a well-worn stone sign indicating 'Ambleside & Skelgill'. Approximately 400m after this is a signposted public bridleway to Ambleside and Skelgill to the left, forking off the main wall-lined track known as Hundreds Road. Take this public bridleway to the left through rolling sheep pasture. Splash through the small **ford** above Lower Skelgill and continue over more open fell, passing a derelict barn to the left about 100m from the ford.

ROBIN LANE AND THE TROUTBECK HUNDREDS

The area above Troutbeck, known as the Hundreds, is an urban common, with open access to walkers and horseriders alike. Your route, Robin Lane, is an old drove road high on the hillside above the enclosed fields. Cattle brought down from Galloway in the autumn would be fattened up on the Lakeland farms over the winter before being driven along this route towards Kendal and onward to the markets of Yorkshire and Lancashire.

The origin of the term 'hundreds' is unclear, but here at Troutbeck it refers to three separate parcels of common land, each of which reputedly had its own bull, constable and bridge. Thus, according to one 1876 source, 'by the computation of shrewd wits, the entire parish contains three hundred constables, three hundred bridges, and three hundred bellowing bulls'; to which the cynic of some neighbouring valley added 'and many hundred feuls'.

After a few minutes' walking, the path descends to a bridge over a beck with a prominent oak tree. Go over the bridge and cattle grid and pick up a road, passing a

National Trust gardens and old farm buildings at Townend

hay meadow owned by the National Trust on the left. The route passes through a farmyard and two gates before the road reverts to a wall-lined gravel track. Here there are extensive views out over Lake Windermere, before the path descends into the lush greenery of Skelgill Wood. After 400m a hole in the wall to the left offers a worth-while diversion to the vantage point of **Jenkin Crag**, an excellent place to draw breath.

Return to the main route and continue on and down through the trees, crossing a delightful stone bridge over **Stencher Beck**. Just over the bridge take the path left down the side of the stream, ignoring the one straight ahead that climbs up through the trees. After 100m the path splits; ignore the branch to the left and keep straight ahead. The path here is quite wide and well made, with a wall to the right, and it becomes an access road to several properties passed on the right-hand side. Continue downhill, with the woods thinning out to reveal a view of the lake. Stay on this main track toward Ambleside. Shortly the spire of St Mary's Church in Ambleside comes into view, and the track drops down into the back of Ambleside behind the Mountain Rescue Base. ◀

Turn right when you hit the tarmac road, Old Lake Road. This will take you into the centre of **Ambleside**, and is a much quieter and walker friendly route than the main A591 that bears the tourist traffic into the town, visible through the houses.

Accommodation:
If you are already seeking to break the journey, turn left here for Ambleside YH, or continue on the route for 0.5km for Ambleside Backpackers hostel.

FURTHER EXPLORATION

Short Walk 2 to Stock Ghyll and High Sweden Bridge takes 2½ hours and leaves from the centre of Ambleside.

FACILITIES

Accommodation

Windermere/Troutbeck
There are a multitude of **hotels** and **B&B** establishments in Windermere – contact Windermere TIC on (015394) 46491 for listings. For **hostels** try Windermere YH, tel: (0870) 7706095, a large hostel in peaceful surroundings with great views over the lake. Beware of the name 'Windermere' – the hostel is some distance out of town in the Troutbeck valley (NY405013), but close to your route. For accommodation in town, at the start of the walk, the Windermere Backpackers, tel: (015394) 46374, is better placed – on the High Street near the station.

Ambleside
For **youth hostels** try Ambleside YH (NY377030), which has double and family rooms, tel: (0870) 7705673, or Ambleside Backpackers (independent) hostel (NY378039), tel: (015394) 32340. Both hostels are at the Waterhead end of town.

Ambleside boasts numerous **B&Bs**, particularly in Compston Road area. Ring Ambleside TIC on (015394) 32582 for information.

Refreshments
Ambleside is a good place to take a break, with numerous coffee shops, pubs and bakeries. It is also one of the main places in the Lake District to stock up on outdoor gear.

Transport
Ambleside and Windermere are well served by the 555 bus route. Buses leave Ambleside from the bus stop opposite the library, and depart Windermere from the front steps of the railway station.

STAGE 2
Ambleside to Elterwater

Distance	5 miles (8km)
Time	2½hrs
Total ascent	245m (800ft)
Maps	OS 1:25,000 OL7, Harvey Superwalker Central sheet
Start point	Ambleside, NY377045
Accommodation	Ambleside, Elterwater
Refreshments	Ambleside, Skelwith Bridge, Elterwater

Ambleside, the starting point for Stage 2, is a lively and compact town, nestled between mountains and lake in an almost Alpine-like setting. Its strategic location led the Romans to build a fort by the lake at Waterhead, but it was the Norse–Irish farmers who really saw the potential here and founded a settlement in the 10th century.

A second wave of prosperity began in the medieval period. For several centuries afterwards the town's fortunes thrived, based on the wool trade. At its peak Ambleside had up to eighteen mills in operation, producing flour, cloth and bobbins (the latter for the Lancashire cotton industry).

The tourist industry took a little while to reach Ambleside – the inaccessibility of the central lakes area prior to the arrival of the turnpike road in 1761 would have required a determined traveller on a packhorse to get to the town. But since the mid-18th century Ambleside has been wedded to tourism – and has never looked back.

On leaving the town, the route goes over Loughrigg Fell and into the heart of the Lake District on easy-to-follow trails, with spectacular views. Throughout this stage you are surrounded by fells and water. Fells with evocative names such as Coniston Old Man, Wetherlam and Pike o'Stickle form the backdrop to this stage, whilst in the foreground water is very much the theme. You'll see Windermere lake from Loughrigg, pass the lily-covered Loughrigg tarn, continue on to the frothy waters of Skelwith, and finish by the tranquil waters of Elterwater, journey's end for the day.

Find the old **market hall** (now housing a restaurant) next to Barclays Bank. Opposite this, walk through The Slack, a small lane that leads downwards to Compston Road. Cross the road to the Walnut Fish Bar before taking the dead-end Vicarage Road to **Rothay Park**, passing St Mary's parish church on the left. Continue through the park on the main path and go over a small iron **foot-bridge** before crossing the beautiful arched stone bridge to the tarred road. Turn right along this road in the direction of Grasmere, crossing a **cattle grid**. After 100m pick up a bridleway to the left taking you uphill along a tarmac road that zigzags upwards between two properties. Keep on this bridleway ignoring a signed footpath to Clappersgate on a corner.

Leaving Ambleside for Elterwater, Loughrigg Tarn is seen from the fell above

51

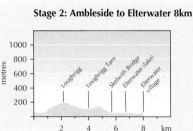

Stage 2: Ambleside to Elterwater 8km

ROMAN AMBLESIDE

Waterhead, or Galava to the Romans, is the oldest part of Ambleside. The spectacular site, under the shadow of the fells at the head of the lake, was first excavated by Robin Collingwood. Between 1913 and 1920 he uncovered a second-century Roman fort overlying an earlier turf and timber structure. Collingwood found stone built granaries, a hypocaust (type of heating system) and barracking for 500 men. Ploughing over the centuries has left little to see above ground today, although shards of Roman pottery still resurface regularly. Ambleside museum houses several artefacts from the site, but Galava itself is well worth a visit simply to admire the views or take in a Windermere sunset.

Go through two gates, and the road turns into a rocky track climbing gently to a third gate, to the left of which, set into the dry-stone wall, is a slate sign indicating Loughrigg, Langdale and Elterwater straight ahead. Go through the gate. The track shortly starts to descend to a stream crossing. Boulder-hop across the water, beyond which point the track forks. **Take the track to the left** – the smaller path ahead leads through the hillside bracken to the summit of Loughrigg and on to Grasmere. Your track narrows and weaves through the bracken. Over the brow, the village of Skelwith Bridge comes into view. Ignore the gate in front, and continue as the sign suggests to the tarn.

The track goes down to a gate with a sign indicating Elterwater, before becoming more loose and rocky as it descends through the trees. Around the corner is a gate to the right with a footpath sign on it. Take this to a second gate at the other side of the field. **Loughrigg Tarn** comes into view. Go over the stile to a well-made track. Turn right and almost immediately left over a second stile. Continue on a well-used path across the field and through a gate, and turn left along a stone-pitched track. After 20m turn off this track to the left onto a marked footpath which leads through the fields at the head of the tarn to join a tarred **side road**.

Turn left here. After 150m take a path to the right, with a fingerpost indicating Skelwith Bridge, that starts as a tarred road but becomes a grass track. The path goes over a stile into the coniferous woods of **Neaum Crag**, then joins a tarred road which leads through the wooden chalets. Continue downward following the yellow public

The distinctive profile of the Langdale Pikes, seen from Loughrigg Fell

Refreshments:
As well as the Talbot Arms, Skelwith Bridge also offers Chesters, a cafe by the river with a good line in home baking.

footpath signs to join the main Langdale Road opposite the **Talbot Arms** at Skelwith Bridge. ◄

On reaching the road turn left, and walk the 200m to the junction of the Coniston Road (**A593**). Turn right in the direction of Coniston for 100m, and at the **river** take the riverside footpath marked 'Elterwater'. Go past the picnic benches and Chesters cafe, then pass through the Kirkstone Slate workshops, with the river now close by on the left. From here a level, well-made footpath leads past Colwith Force waterfall and **Elterwater lake** before reaching **Elterwater** village.

THE LANGUAGE OF THE LAKES

Of all the travellers and settlers in the Lake District, it is undoubtedly the Vikings that left the biggest linguistic mark on the region, at least in terms of the number of their place names and geographical terms still in everyday use. Some of the best known are below, and have been assimilated into the English language.

thwaite (*thweit*)	clearing	as in Stonethwaite
fell (*fjall*)	hill	as in The Lakeland Fells
force (*fors*)	waterfall	as in Scale Force (waterfall by the hut)
gill / ghyll (*gil*)	ravine	as in Rosgill (ravine of the horses)
beck (*bekkr*)	stream	as in Stonethwaite Beck

Other Norse-derived geographical terms include pike (angular peak), hause (pass between hills), rigg (ridge) and wath (ford). Individual Norse settlers also left their names on the landscape – Ullswater is named after Ulf, Windermere after Vinard, and Coniston (or Thurston Water as it used to be known) after Thursteinn. A Norseman named Huni also apparently had his summer pasture (*saetr*) at today's Honister.

Old English also provides some geographical terms – 'mere', for example, being the pool by the good grazing ground referred to in 'Buttermere', but Norse is the language of the fells. Except, that is, in the business of counting sheep. Many Cumbrian school-children can use the local dialect words used to count up to ten sheep – yan, tyan, tehera, methera, pimp, sethera, lethera, hovera, dovera, dick – in Borrowdale, for example, but this system has no link with Norse whatsoever. Apparently pre-dating the Norse shep-herds, instead it is related to the Celtic tongues of Wales, Cornwall and Brittany.

A former farmhouse, the youth hostel at Elterwater is found a few yards beyond the village green

FURTHER EXPLORATION

Short Walk 3, a circular route from Elterwater down the Langdale valley, takes 3¼ hours, and is a good option for an afternoon stroll.

FACILITIES

Accommodation and food

Facilities in **Ambleside** are given in the box at the end of Stage 1.

Elterwater

This small village has a limited number of accommodation providers. At the budget end, Elterwater YH (NY327047), housed in a former farmhouse near the centre of the village, has small rooms as well as dormitory space – tel: (015394) 36293, elterwater@yha.org.uk.

Also in the centre of the village, the Britannia Inn (NY328048) – tel: (015394) 37210, www.britinn.co.uk – has rooms and a restaurant, with regional specialities on the menu.

The more expensive Eltermere Country House Hotel (NY327045), a little further along the lane from the youth hostel, looks out toward the lake – tel: (015394) 37207, www.eltermere.co.uk – and finally for four-star accommodation there is The Langdale Hotel (NY326053), tel: (015394) 37302 www.langdale.co.uk.

All the above serve evening meals.

In nearby **Chapel Stile** Wainwrights Inn serves bar meals, and Brambles cafe is open during the day for breakfasts and lunchtime snacks.

Transport

Elterwater is served by the 516 bus service from Ambleside. The service is daily, but infrequent. Catch the bus from the stop just opposite the Britannia Inn, by the National Trust car park.

STAGE 3
Elterwater to Coniston

Distance	6 miles (9.5km)
Time	2½hrs
Total ascent	250m (830ft)
Maps	OS 1:25,000 OL7, Harvey Superwalker South East and Central sheets
Start point	Elterwater village, NY328048
Accommodation	Elterwater, Coniston
Refreshments	Elterwater, Little Langdale, Coniston

Elterwater (from the Norse for 'swan lake') guards the entrance to the Langdale valley, a playground for hillwalkers and climbers, and deservedly popular with visitors for much of the year. The Tour heads past on slightly quieter routes, first into Little Langdale before continuing through Tilberthwaite to Coniston.

If your itinerary permits, a stop-over day in Elterwater is very worthwhile – a pleasant riverside stroll or a hike up the Langdale Pikes that dominate the head of the valley are all possible from here. Now firmly devoted to tourism, Elterwater still maintains a working slate mine, and it is worth a peek from the nearby footpath into the vast hole in the ground just to marvel at the scale of operations.

The geology of the valley has been worked for millennia – the Langdale Pikes was an 'axe factory' in Neolithic times, producing axe rough-outs that still appear in the screes today. Axes originating from Langdale rock have been found in other parts of Britain and abroad. In the 1990s further links to prehistory were uncovered with the discovery of ancient man-made markings on two boulders at Copt Howe, 20 minutes' walk from Elterwater.

From the **Britannia** pub follow the road past the National Trust car park on your left, over the bridge, passing a row of pretty cottages on your right. One of these, formerly a farmhouse, now houses the youth hostel. Shortly after the Eltermere Country House Hotel pick up the lane to the right, and after 100m pass **Elterwater Hall**. The lane climbs uphill for a further 150m before splitting into two.

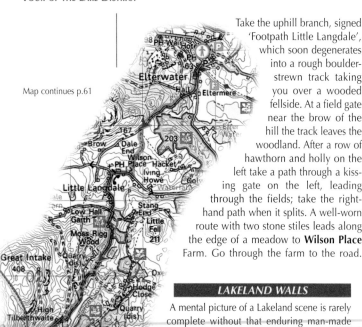

Map continues p.61

Take the uphill branch, signed 'Footpath Little Langdale', which soon degenerates into a rough boulder-strewn track taking you over a wooded fellside. At a field gate near the brow of the hill the track leaves the woodland. After a row of hawthorn and holly on the left take a path through a kissing gate on the left, leading through the fields; take the right-hand path when it splits. A well-worn route with two stone stiles leads along the edge of a meadow to **Wilson Place** Farm. Go through the farm to the road.

LAKELAND WALLS

A mental picture of a Lakeland scene is rarely complete without that enduring man-made adornment, the dry-stone wall. From the fields around the region's lowland villages to the summits of England's highest peak they are seldom absent, marking and dividing the landscape into man-made and manageable sections.

Enduring they may be (for a well-constructed dry-stone wall might be expected to last a century or more without restoration) but for the most part they are not ancient. The greatest period of construction was in the late 18th and early 19th centuries, and most of what we see today dates from this time.

Before that time there had been little reason to enclose land. The earliest walls around the Norse farmsteads were small-scale attempts by individual farmers to provide pockets of accessible land distinct from the common pasture, suited to growing

House and field,
Little Langdale

feed or confining their stock when needed. The earliest outlying walls in the fells themselves date from the medieval period, built by the big landowners of the day, the Cistercian abbeys.

The boom in the woollen industry in the 16th and 17th centuries required larger enclosures close to the villages, and this accounts for some of the long, narrow fields reaching out from the villages along the valleys. With time it became necessary to demarcate boundaries of common land between valleys or parishes, hence the long, singular and seemingly purposeless walls in out-of-the-way places in the fells.

The peak of wall-building activity was reached in the early 19th century, following the Enclosure Acts of 1802. Land suitable for sheep husbandry was now a valuable asset, and the legal framework for enclosure, land tenureship and transfer was well established. Wall building now commenced with industrial efficiency, the task of itinerant masons.

Since 1850 wall building has ceased on any real scale, due to a decline in need and affordability. Walls that remain are increasingly regarded as a valuable heritage resource, and through the efforts of individual wallers and organisations such as the National Trust and the British Trust for Conservation Volunteers, their place in the landscape is being preserved.

Throughout the tour you will pass many dry-stone features, not all of them walls. Look out for packhorse bridges, their narrow width a reminder that wheeled transport came late to the north country. Dry-stone walls may have 'hogg holes' built in to the lower section – gates to allow young sheep through to fresh grazing. You may find sheepfolds built near streams to hold the flock for sheep washing, a practice that has now died out. In the days before sheep were dipped in pesticides, they were dunked in the beck to clean the fleece before shearing.

The inn's name celebrates the nearby meeting point of the old county boundaries of Cumberland, Westmorland and Lancashire.

Now in Little Langdale, as opposed to Great Langdale, the route continues right from Wilson Place Farm along the road passing the **Three Shires Inn** on the right. ◄ One hundred metres beyond the Inn, take the first lane on the left signed 'Tilberthwaite – unsuitable for motor vehicles'. The lane leads down to a **ford** in the River Brathay. Cross with the footbridge, initially veering leftwards once over the river, keeping on the main track. At the hairpin in the track, 100m from the bridge over the Brathay, keep to the right-hand track by the wall. Follow this track for 2km, passing spoil from the slate quarries. Now in the Tilberthwaite area, you pass through a wooded section, punctuated with evidence of slate mining. Keep on through the woodland and through a field gate with a kissing gate next to it, at which point the track leaves the woodland, shortly

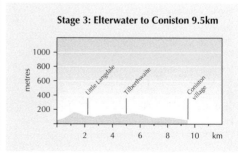

Stage 3: Elterwater to Coniston 9.5km

reaching the farm at **Tilberthwaite**. From here take the tarred lane leading out of the valley toward Coniston. ▶

Don't miss Andy Goldsworthy's artistic take on the sheepfold, to the left as you pass a parking area.

MINING IN THE TILBERTHWAITE AND CONISTON AREA

Coniston's fortunes were found in the fells – slate from quarries at Tilberthwaite and under the Old Man, and copper from the Coppermines valley high above the village. Today's pound may be earned from tourism, but the green roofs and solidly built slate cottages and villas are a link to earlier labours. Slate quarries were first recorded in the 17th century, but copper mining has been going on in the area since the Bronze Age, and there is evidence of larger scale extraction in Roman times too.

Greater exploitation in the area dates from the very end of the 16th century. Copper ore extracted by the German mining company of Keswick (see Stage 8) was taken by packhorse back up to Brigham near Keswick for smelting. Copper mining at Coniston reached its peak of production in the mid-19th century, when the Coniston Mining Company employed 400 men. Coniston Coppermines YH is housed in one of the former copper mining buildings – a search around outside will reveal settling tanks, spoil heaps and part of the old crusher.

In the 21st century copper may have had its day, but here (as at Elterwater and Honister) slate mining is still ongoing.

61

Coniston village and lake, seen from near Brantwood on the eastern shore

On reaching the **Ambleside–Coniston road** turn right, but at the signpost pick up the 'Footpath Coniston 1½ miles' just to the right of the road, which makes for more pleasant walking through the trees on a level path to the outskirts of **Coniston** by Holly How Youth Hostel. For Coniston village take the lane downhill, and for Coniston Coppermines Youth Hostel continue along the path behind Holly How which leads to the Coppermines track.

FURTHER EXPLORATION

Short Walk 4, from Coniston village to Ruskin's former home at Brantwood, can be adapted for a short evening outing or a full day out.

FACILITIES

Accommodation
Facilities in **Elterwater** are given in the box at the end of Stage 2.

Coniston
There are numerous small **hotels** and **B&Bs** in the village – contact Tourist Information on (015394) 41533. Coniston is usually reasonably priced for accommodation. Two noteworthy B&Bs are The Beech Tree (specialising in vegetarian food) and Bank Ground Farm (for its Arthur Ransome associations).

The two **hostels** in the YHA network mentioned in the route description above can be contacted on (015394) 41261 for Coniston Coppermines and (015394) 41323 for Holly How.

Campers need to walk a mile or so down the lake shore to Coniston Hall **campsite** (SD304959), operated by the National Trust, tel: (015394) 41223.

Food
Food is rather less plentiful in Coniston in the evening – the numerous daytime cafes in the village tend to leave evening meals to the pubs, but with spots like the Sun Inn and Black Bull it's not too much of a problem.

Transport
The 505/506 Coniston Rambler bus service to Hawkshead and Ambleside passes through Coniston's main street.

STAGE 4
Coniston to Eskdale

Distance	11 miles (17.5km)
Time	4½–6½hrs
Ascent	880m (2880ft)
Maps	OS 1:25,000 OL6, Harvey Superwalker South West sheet
Start point	Coniston village, SD303976
Accommodation	Coniston, Eskdale
Refreshments	Woolpack Inn, Boot village
High-level alternative	from Coniston to Eskdale via the Old Man and Hardknott (see Part 3, High Level 1)

Coniston, our starting point is replete with literary associations. John Ruskin made his home over the water at Brantwood, and the Coniston area later inspired Arthur Ransome, who based several of his 'Swallows and Amazons' books on locations in and around Coniston. Ransome himself lived for a time at Nibthwaite at the far end of the lake.

More recently Coniston has become known as the lake where in 1967 Donald Campbell made his doomed attempt on the water speed record in 'Bluebird'. The wreckage of the 'Bluebird' was salvaged in spring 2001, and Campbell finally given a proper funeral in the autumn. At the time of writing, Campbell's daughter is attempting to secure funds to allow the 'Bluebird' to be restored and exhibited in Coniston's Ruskin Museum. Today you can enjoy a snack at the Bluebird Cafe, situated on the lake shore, from where a launch leaves for Brantwood. Real ale enthusiasts might choose instead to head for the Black Bull Inn a pint of Coniston Bluebird Bitter.

From Coniston the fourth stage of the tour follows the old Walna Scar route over to the peaceful Duddon valley, before climbing again over the mossy fell to Eskdale, our destination for the day. At 11 miles, it is one of the longer stages of the tour. The walking is generally easy, with no steep climbing. Two gradual ascents, Walna Scar in the morning and Ulpha Fell in the afternoon, surprisingly total almost 900m of ascent.

Between leaving Coniston and touching down in Eskdale by the Woolpack Inn the route shies clear of habitation – you will need to take supplies of food and drink with you. For accommodation in Eskdale when you arrive, most options other than the Woolpack and the youth hostel are in the little village of Boot, one mile further on from the Woolpack Inn.

There is a high-level alternative to this stage, which takes in Coniston Old Man for just a little extra effort at the beginning of the day. It then continues on undemanding terrain to Eskdale, on less used footpaths. The high-level route is rewarding in fine weather for its spectacular views – although the main route has better marked footpaths.

From **Coniston** village centre cross the bridge by Barclays Bank, passing the offices of Coniston Coppermines Holiday Cottages and reach the petrol station. Take the lane almost opposite the petrol station winding up the hill, passing to the right of the old railway station. This is sadly no longer in operation, but instead put to use as light industrial units. Keep on this main lane which leads on to the Walna Scar road, an old route from Coniston to Eskdale – it's a steep pull up here to wake you up in the morning! In an age of road and motorway building it's curious to see a road fall into disuse – the route was driveable by motor cars 30 years ago, but has been allowed to decline. Four-wheel drive enthusiasts still relish the challenge, but nowadays it's very much a mountain bike and walking trail.

THE OLD RAILWAY

Coniston had its own railway station until 1957, a branch from the west coast line from Broughton. Built in 1857, it was primarily used to transport copper out from the mines above the town. As the track coincided with the new wave of railway tourism the route was initially successful, but by the twilight years of the 19th century it had started to struggle. The cessation of mining activities, and the station's distance above the town and lake, meant it ultimately failed to survive on passenger transport alone.

A winding track in Dunnerdale, typical of the old enclosed lanes

As the lane levels out it reaches the Walna Scar car park, a favourite departure point for walkers bound for the Old Man of Coniston, which you can see to the right. Proceed through the car park between the two wooden gate posts marking the start of the **Walna Scar road** and offering information about off-road driving etiquette. A little further on beyond the last of the walled fields, 400m from the car park, a footpath to the Old Man leads off the main Scar track to the right. Ignore this and continue onwards. The track is clear and easy to follow – this being a route used for centuries to link the valleys. Further on, as it rounds the southern flank of the **Old Man**, the track crosses an old packhorse bridge and heads to its highest point, a pass just to the southwest of **Brown Pike**.

About 1½hrs after leaving Coniston, the top of the Walna Scar track is reached, and the view into Dunnerdale opens up beneath. The descent into Dunnerdale is straightforward, and the **Walna Scar** track, which you follow, is distinct. To the right the profile of Harter Fell marks the head of the valley and serves as a reference point for the next part of the day, when the route goes into the forest on its southeastern flank before traversing the southwestern fellside into Eskdale.

First though, wind down the last of the Walna Scar track to meet the end of Dunnerdale's tarred road. Once on the tarred road turn right over a small bridge, go through a gate and into a field, then go through a second field gate opening before turning left to pick up a footpath through a small gate by the edge of a wood. Reaching this gate requires traversing a boggy area – but in summer there are lots of interesting marsh plants to look at – cotton grass, sphagnum mosses, sundews and the like. Once through this small gate, a lonnin takes you to a farm called **Long House**. Follow the waymarked path through the farm buildings. As you come through the gardens of this pretty farm, a short dog-leg right brings you to a signpost directing you into a second lonnin.

Cross three fields to **Tongue House** Farm. Walk into the farmyard, and at the white house pass left through a green metal field gate onto a tarred track which you follow before crossing a wooden **footbridge** over a beck. The path now goes diagonally across the

Map continues p.69

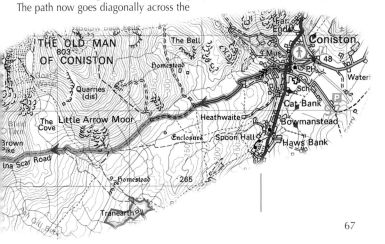

field, passing in front of another pretty white farmhouse onto a delightful single-track path that meanders into riverside woodland. The path forks 50m beyond the white house. Take the left-hand fork to climb upwards through the trees before crossing over an old dry-stone wall and into bracken. Keep on this path, with Harter Fell ahead of you, to meet the road.

At the road turn right and go over a cattle grid, continuing to **Troutall** Farm, a B&B establishment. At the farm, turn left onto a footpath leading through fields to a footbridge over a beck. Once over the footbridge, take the permissive path to the left by the River Duddon, and follow it downstream through predominantly coniferous woodland. ◀

A little care is needed in places here. In some parts the going is very boggy; in others care is required when crossing sometimes greasy boulders.

As it nears the end of the wood, the path splashes across a beck 20m beneath a waterfall – a great place to stop for a breather. Shortly afterwards you see **stepping stones** crossing the River Duddon with a fixed-wire handrail. At this point turn right, uphill, along the bridleway. Now you're amidst beech and birch trees, with the tumbling waters of **Grassguards Gill** audible to the left. Reaching Grassguards Farm on the bridleway, a footpath leads over to the southwest bank of Grassguards Gill, which you follow upstream on another bridleway flanked by a dry-stone wall on the left.

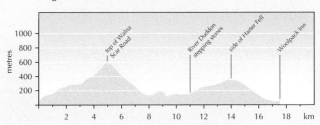

Stage 4: Coniston to Eskdale 17.5km

The way levels out a little at this point, with easier walking on grassy ground. Go over a ladder-stile by a field gate between two stands of conifers, and continue straight ahead through a smaller field gate. Now in marshy ground, continue upwards. Nearing the top of the plantation, to your left a finger post indicates a bridleway on the right. Take this, crossing over a little stream through a defunct gate, still climbing gently upwards. **Ulpha Fell** is now on the left, and **Harter Fell** on the right.

In time the path levels out, but it is a very muddy squelch up here as you go over the watershed into Eskdale. After crossing a forestry fence through a small wooden gate it does get a little drier, moving into bracken and rough grassland. At SD207 997 a stile appears on the fence you have been following for some time, behind which, to the left, is a dry-stone wall hiding

Eskdale and the sea from Hardknott, with the Isle of Man visible beyond the coastline – note the remains of the Roman fort in sunlight to right

Spothow Gill. Take this stile and footpath following a decrepit dry-stone wall for the first few metres. Shortly afterwards the path crosses the beck by stepping stones before continuing downward to Eskdale.

The route down into Eskdale is reasonably obvious, and is cairned in places as it goes through some crags, from where it starts to descend quite sharply down the valley side. The path crosses a beck by a lonely oak tree, and follows a wall gently downhill to a field gate by a sheepfold leading into a field. Keep to the right of the field, picking up a track leading to **Penny Hill Farm**, now in sight. Approaching the farm, take the permitted path to the left signed 'To Doctor Bridge'. Go over **Doctor Bridge**, and follow the lane up to the main Eskdale road. Turn right along the road and continue to the **Woolpack Inn**.

FURTHER EXPLORATION

Short Walk 5, Muncaster Fell and Ravenglass from the Eskdale railway, shows you more of Eskdale if you have the time, and covers the final few miles of the valley to the coast.

FACILITIES

Accommodation and food
Facilities in **Coniston** are given in the box at the end of Stage 3.

Camping
Hollins Farm (+1km; NY178010), tel: (019467) 23288
Small, well-appointed campsite next to Brook House Inn on main road near Boot.

Youth hostel
Eskdale YH (+400m; NY196010), tel: (019467) 23219
Food and accommodation, small rooms available. Near to Woolpack Inn on Hardknott Road.

B&Bs and inns
Burnmoor Inn (+1.5km), tel: (019467) 23224, and Brook House Inn (+1km), tel: (019467) 23288, both at Boot (NY176011), offer food and accommodation.

Eskdale's website, www.eskdale.info, has links to other offers of accommodation.

Transport
Other than 'Ratty', the valley's narrow-gauge railway, Eskdale is not well served by public transport. Dalegarth station near Boot will get you onto Ratty, but unless you want to connect to the west Cumbrian railway line via Ravenglass, a taxi may be the only option if you need to leave Eskdale without walking.

STAGE 5
Eskdale to Wasdale

Distance	7½ miles (12km)
Time	3–4½hrs
Ascent	400m (1300ft)
Maps	OS 1:25,000 OL6, Harvey Superwalker West sheet
Start point	Woolpack Inn, Eskdale, NY190010
Accommodation	Boot, Nether Wasdale
Refreshments	Eskdale Green, Nether Wasdale
High-level alternative	from Eskdale to Wasdale Head via Scafell Pike (see Part 3, High Level 2)

This a day of fine valley walking, tracing the route of the River Esk downstream to Eskdale Green, before a slightly more strenuous traverse of Miterdale's wooded slopes, ending in Wasdale. Quieter than the valleys of the central lakes, this is a peaceful section to enjoy at leisure. Highlights include the small church of St Catherine's tucked away by the riverside, and the Eskdale narrow-gauge railway, which is crossed halfway through the section near Eskdale Green. Miterdale, tucked as it is between the better-known valleys of Eskdale and Wasdale, is a much overlooked gem, and the perfect gateway to the grandeur of Wasdale itself.

You can choose to end the day either at Wasdale Youth Hostel, a grand affair overlooking the lake, or in the village of Nether Wasdale nearby, where there are two inns.

For those seeking something more challenging than this gentle route to Wasdale, there is a high-level alternative (High Level 2) which heads over Scafell Pike from the northeast corner of Eskdale. Whilst not technically difficult, the high-level route is significantly longer and, particularly around the summit area of Scafell Pike, requires competent navigation skills, especially in poor weather. The high-level route is therefore recommended for capable walkers keen to climb Scafell Pike, while the main route is a great opportunity for an effortless exploration of Eskdale.

St Catherine's Church, Eskdale, with its open campanile

From the **Woolpack Inn**, walk 300m down the road in the direction of Eskdale Green before turning left down a no-through road to **Doctor Bridge**. Take the footpath on the near bank signed 'to St Catherine's Church', following the river bank for a short while before running into a lonnin. From here, an obvious path leads through sheep pasture and riverside trees. This is nice, easy, uncomplicated walking just slightly downhill – savour it as the miles slip by underfoot. After a bend in the river look out for a footbridge visible between a gap in the wall. Unless the river is high, don't cross this footbridge (there are stepping stones later on), but keep on the riverside path to reach St Catherine's Church with its twin open campanile (bell tower).

73

ST CATHERINE'S CHURCH

Local legend has it that a sixth-century hermit and healer lived near to the site of St Catherine's Church, his holy well determining the site of the charming, modest church founded in 1125 by William Le Meschines of Egremont Castle. The Victorians restored the church in 1881, but managed to keep much of the church's charm. The font dates back to the 14th century, and the treble bell was cast in 1445. The stepping stones crossing the river are part of an ancient route, being used by worshippers possibly since before the church itself was built.

Cross the river by the stepping stones at the church. If the river is in spate retrace your steps and cross by the footbridge instead. Once over the stepping stones turn right along the bridleway through the birch trees to cross Lucy Norris' footbridge over a tributary stream joining the Esk from the left. Continue on the bridleway, crossing another track to follow the sign 'Forge Bridge and Eskdale Green'. Keep on this well-maintained and easy-to-follow route until the Milkingstead suspension bridge is reached, leading back over the River Esk. Take the footpath over the bridge, and go through the field to the road.

Stage 5: Eskdale to Wasdale 12km

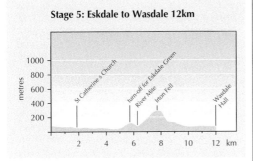

On meeting the Eskdale road, cross over into Fisherground campsite. Follow the signed footpath through the grounds briefly before picking up the permitted path to the left, avoiding **Fisherground farmyard**, and rejoin the footpath through a field gate at the far side of the farm buildings. The footpath continues up along a lonnin to some sheepfolds. Here, go through the field gate and dog-leg left over the tracks of the **Eskdale to Ravenglass railway**. Take care crossing the line.

ESKDALE TO RAVENGLASS RAILWAY

Fifteen inches wide and seven miles long, the tracks of the Eskdale to Ravenglass railway cut a route from Dalegarth, a little further up the valley, down through Miterdale to meet the coast. Completed in 1875 to carry iron ore out to the main coast line, financial irregularities meant that within two years it was in the hands of the receiver. The mining operations fared little better, and were soon abandoned, thus leaving 'laal Ratty' to seek a fortune carrying tourist passengers through the pretty valley.

Travelling on Ratty in the Victorian years must have been a hair-raising experience. With no money available for its upkeep, maintenance and safety standards were poor – but, thankfully, travelling speed was a sedate five miles per hour, maintained apparently with a helping push from passengers on the uphill sections!

It was not until the 1960s that Ratty's future was secured; now it is lovingly cherished by a band of dedicated enthusiasts and enjoyed by thousands of visitors per year.

Beyond the railway tracks, the footpath enters an ash and birch woodland. As you leave the woodland and move into more open rough pasture, a track cuts straight across yours; keep straight ahead. Shortly afterwards, after passing through a new field gate in a wall, climb gently over a bracken-covered fellside with woodland on your left. After going over the brow of the hill, pass through a field gate leading into a lonnin heading downhill. After 50m a crossroads is reached. Decision time – if you want to make a small diversion to seek refreshments in the village of **Eskdale Green** turn left, otherwise turn right. The track heads uphill with a wall to the left, passing a picturesque small farm **at Low Holme**. From here the track leads downhill to a quiet lane. Cross straight over to pick up a bridleway to Nether Wasdale, via Miterdale.

Near the start of the bridleway, once over the little packhorse bridge by the bridleway sign, veer towards the left. The bridleway is fairly easy to follow, except where tracks cut across the main bridleway's route: when you meet the first of these dog-leg left and keep heading up. Again, when you encounter a second track crossing yours, go straight across and up. At a third track, dog-leg right and continue up to a wooden bench. From here, keep onwards and upwards crossing any tracks you find. Eventually, amidst the conifers, the track finally levels out and you realize that you are at the top.

Emerging from the trees you enter a new valley – Wasdale. Continue straight ahead over the fell. Sellafield is the distinctive landmark on the coast to the left; more appealingly, the greens of the Wasdale valley open up on the right, though Wastwater itself has yet to make an appearance. As you work down Irton Fell Wastwater, with its scree-flanked walls, finally reveals itself. At the base **of Irton Fell**, go through a small gate in the wall onto a forest bridleway, and follow this for 200m to reach a wooden signpost. ▶

Turn right onto a public footpath bordered by forest on the right and a dry-stone wall on the left. Continue following the wall through a kissing gate to **Easthwaite** Farm, taking a footpath just before the farm buildings and passing through another kissing gate at the corner of the field. From here head right through the bottom of the farm to find a footpath signed 'Wasdale Head' along a farm track. With the sound of a beck bubbling in your left ear, a footpath meets your track, coming in at an oblique angle from the left.

Accommodation and refreshment: If you want to go into Nether Wasdale for accommodation or refreshment go straight on here. To return to the main route afterwards, take the road to the lake, picking up the description at Wasdale Hall, the start point of Stage 6.

Wastwater reflections, an almost perfect mirror image on a calm day

Meeting the footpath, it's decision time again – which side of the lake to take? The western side, along the screes, is hard going on the loose ground; the eastern side necessitates road walking – but is rewarded with views of the screes themselves. The route described below and in Stage 6 is the road route. Generally, the road is recommended except at weekends and peak holiday times when the traffic is too great for relaxing walking. At these times you would be advised to continue along the track to the screes, and follow the alternate route described in Stage 6.

For the road route, take the footpath to the woodlands by the beck. After 300m cross an old stone bridge before heading right through a kissing gate on a permissive path. The path follows the beck back to the lake, and continues on by the lake shore to **Wasdale Hall** – now a youth hostel.

FACILITIES

Facilities in **Boot** are given in the box at the end of Stage 4.

Accommodation

Camping
Continue on to Wasdale Head on Stage 6 to the National Trust campsite (+3½ miles; NY183075), tel. (019467) 26220.

Youth hostel
YHA Wastwater at Wasdale Hall (NY145045), on the route, by the lake shore, tel. (019467) 26222

Inns and B&Bs
The Strands, tel: (019467) 26237, and The Screes, tel: (019467) 26262, both in Nether Wasdale (NY126040), offer food and accommodation. Other options may be found from www.wasdaleweb.co.uk.

Transport
Like neighbouring Eskdale, Wastwater gets a raw deal with bus services. However, a taxi-bus service operates on Thursdays, Saturdays and Sundays. Book before 6pm on the day before travel with Gosforth Taxis on (019467) 25308.

STAGE 6
Wasdale to Black Sail

Distance	7 miles (11.5km)
Time	3½–4½hrs (main route)
Ascent	595m (1950ft)
Map	OS 1:25,000 OL6, OL4;
	Harvey Superwalker West sheet
Start point	Wasdale Hall, NY145045
Accommodation	Wasdale Head, Black Sail, Ennerdale
Refreshments	Wasdale Head
High-level alternative	from Wasdale Head to Black Sail (end of Stage 6)
	or Buttermere (end of Stage 7) via Great Gable
	(see Part 3, High Level 3)

This short section is concerned entirely with Wasdale, and if any of the Lakeland valleys deserves a chapter to itself, it is surely this one. The geography textbooks highlight Wastwater as the deepest of the lakes, yet it is the unbroken and unforgiving scree-flanked walls of the valley to the southwest that lend it scale and shape its character. To savour a still evening in the valley, with the late sun catching the screes, is an unforgettable experience – to a photographer the lure of a perfect reflection on the water will prove irresistible.

Wasdale, like its neighbour Ennerdale to the north, is almost entirely defined by nature – man is mercifully absent: beyond Wasdale Hall one road leads to a handful of farms, two campsites, a pub and little else. As befits the valley under England's highest peak, the people of Wasdale are a hardy breed – the most famous and enduring of fell runners, Joss Naylor, is a Wasdale resident, and the Wasdale Head Inn has been the bar of choice for Lakeland climbers since the sport came to the Lakeland crags.

As outlined in Stage 5 the main route, described below, heads along the lake by the road, and the route via the screes is outlined as an alternative. The first half of the main route is flat, easy walking. The hard work comes later, with the traverse from Mosedale over Black Sail pass. Note that the end of this stage, Black Sail, is no more than a small, isolated youth hostel at the head of Ennerdale. If you are lucky enough to secure a reservation, a night here amidst the mountains is well worthwhile. Alternatively you might choose to follow the River Liza downstream to Gillerthwaite in Ennerdale for accommodation, or continue walking Stage 7 to Buttermere, as described in the next chapter.

Packhorse bridge, Wasdale Head, behind the inn, for centuries a place of rest and refreshment

The lakeside path by **Wasdale Hall** runs onto the Wasdale Head road, which you must now follow for three miles towards Wasdale Head. (For the alternative route via the screes, see section below.) A little beyond the head of the lake, as you pass the entrance to the National Trust **campsite**, the white gable end of the Wasdale Head Inn comes into sight; at this point look out for a footpath to the left of the road signed to 'Wasdale Head'. This takes you through beckside fields to a packhorse bridge at the back of the **Wasdale Head Inn**. If not overnighting at the inn or campsite, a pint and snack here is not a bad idea. Apart from the opportunity to take in the climbing ambience of this bar adorned with photographs of past and present aficionados, Wasdale Head is also the last refuelling point before Buttermere – unless of course you have booked a stay at Black Sail. There's also a shop next door selling outdoor gear, useful if you've left something crucial at home. ◀

Note: for those taking the high-level route to Buttermere, leave the main route at Wasdale Head – turn to Part 3, High Level 3, for your route description.

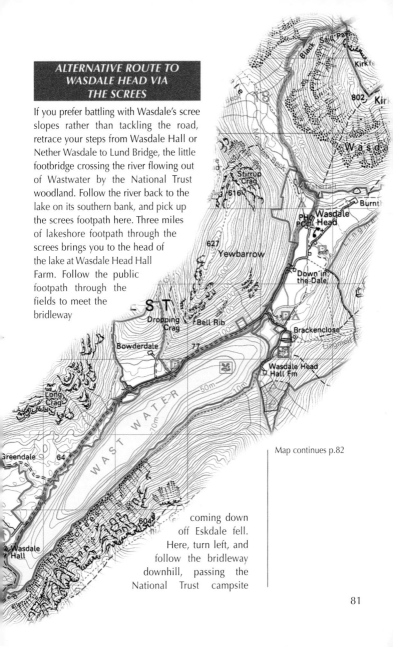

If you prefer battling with Wasdale's scree slopes rather than tackling the road, retrace your steps from Wasdale Hall or Nether Wasdale to Lund Bridge, the little footbridge crossing the river flowing out of Wastwater by the National Trust woodland. Follow the river back to the lake on its southern bank, and pick up the screes footpath here. Three miles of lakeshore footpath through the screes brings you to the head of the lake at Wasdale Head Hall Farm. Follow the public footpath through the fields to meet the bridleway

coming down off Eskdale fell. Here, turn left, and follow the bridleway downhill, passing the National Trust campsite

Map continues p.82

before rejoining the main route on the road to Wasdale Head.

Before leaving Wasdale Head en route to Black Sail, consider a short detour to St Olaf's Church – the footpath is almost opposite the inn by the campsite.

Reputedly the smallest church in England it is certainly dwarfed by the surrounding fells. Carved into the wood inside the door, an apt inscription reads 'I will lift up mine eyes unto the hills'.

HERDWICKS AND VIKINGS

Back in the 10th century, a group of pioneering travellers came to Wasdale. Arriving from the west by sea, these Norsefolk were not the warring Vikings of familiar stereotype; more likely they were simply travellers in search of new land to cultivate and a new life. In Wasdale they would have found a sparsely populated, thickly forested valley, a wildwood still littered with the debris of the glaciers. Today, evidence of their habitation here can be found in the many Norse place names on the Ordnance Survey map of the area.

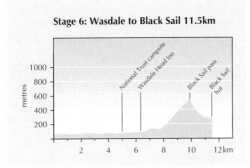

Stage 6: Wasdale to Black Sail 11.5km

The lineage of the Herdwick sheep in the Lake District is subject to conjecture. The name and breed is certainly at least as old as the medieval period, but the original progenitors may well have been brought over in the Norse boats of the 10th century.

To continue on the route to Black Sail, take the path at the side of the Wasdale Head Inn for 25m back to the packhorse bridge crossed earlier, but this time keep on the pub side of the beck and head up the bridleway

Herdwicks standing in line after shearing at Wasdale Head

signed 'Black Sail pass'. With the mass of Kirkfell in front of you guarding the top of Wasdale, the bridleway now veers northwest, continuing into **Mosedale**. As Kirkfell with Gable behind it marked the head of the main valley of Wasdale, you now face Pillar, a forbidding rocky fell claiming this subsidiary valley of Mosedale as its own.

The route continues up Mosedale, seemingly to end under Pillar, but in fact it hooks right to discover a pass between Pillar and Kirkfell. Initially it's an easy, level stroll along the valley floor, but with some climbing later as it heads north and up, following the beck to the col of **Black Sail pass**.

St Olaf's Church, Wasdale Head, one of England's smallest

With the ascent started, the track splashes over **Gatherstone Beck** and continues upwards, looping away from the waters for a short while. The last push to the top is stone-pitched in places, but be prepared for the odd scramble. A cairn marks the top of the pass, and you cross a defunct iron boundary fence before descending into **Ennerdale**.

The path down into the head of Ennerdale is distinct, but care is needed on the way down, especially when wet – the stones polished by the multitudes can get slippery. Once clear of the boulders, the path heads through the drumlins – the grass-covered mounds of glacial drift. A footbridge leads on to **Black Sail Youth Hostel**, a simple single-storey former shepherd's hut, which since the 1930s has been a much-used and much-loved youth hostel amidst the high fells.

FACILITIES

Accommodation and supplies

Wasdale Head

Camping
National Trust Campsite (NY183075), tel. (019467) 26220
Barn Door Shop and Campsite, by the Wasdale Head Inn (NY187087), tel. (019467) 26229

Inns and B&Bs
Wasdale Head Inn, tel. (019467) 26229
Lingmell House B&B, tel. (019467) 26261
Burnthwaite Farm B&B (+800m; NY193091), tel. (019467) 26242

Ennerdale
Black Sail YH (NY195124), tel. (07711) 108450
Ennerdale YH (NY142141), at Gillerthwaite (+3 miles), tel. (01946) 861237
Shepherd's Barn (camping barn), also at Gillerthwaite, tel. (01946) 758198

Transport
From Wasdale Head – see Stage 5
From Black Sail – none

STAGE 7
Black Sail to Buttermere

Distance	4 miles (6km)
Time	1½hrs
Ascent	240m (780ft)
Maps	OS 1:25,000 OL4, Harvey Superwalker West sheet
Start point	Black Sail YH, NY195124
Accommodation	Black Sail YH; Buttermere – campsite, hotels, youth hostel
Refreshments	Tea rooms and pubs in Buttermere village
High-level alternative	Black Sail to Buttermere (see Part 3, High Level 3)

This is the shortest section of the Tour. It is not intended as a day's walk in itself, but is likely to be combined with either Stage 6 (creating a journey from Wasdale to Buttermere) or with Stage 8 (Black Sail to Keswick). At Black Sail the route briefly enters the valley of Ennerdale, at its most southerly and remote end where the River Liza gathers her waters from the flanks of Great Gable and Pillar. Black Sail hut, the starting point for Stage 7, has become something of a legend amongst youth hostellers over the years. As you pass, you may find the door open – cups of tea are sometimes available for a donation. The walls of this modest stone building have echoed with tales from the hills since it was first opened as a youth hostel in the 1930s.

Once alive with human activity – the work of coppicers, iron workers, shepherds – the Ennerdale valley is now a place to savour something akin to wilderness. Black Sail hut, a former shepherd's bothy, sits on a site probably used as a summer shieling for centuries – today the sheep are tended by farmers who commute in by Land Rover.

From the hut, your route weaves up through Scarth Gap, the pass between Haystacks and the High Stile range to the north. An interesting descent into the Buttermere valley continues through lakeshore woodland to Buttermere village itself. With two inns, a cafe, a campsite and a youth hostel, the village is a good stopping-off point for the night.

*Black Sail and
Ennerdale in winter –
complete solitude*

Leaving **Black Sail hut**, turn away from the hills and head
west towards the sea, along the track to cross a beck 20m
away. Follow the rough track downhill for 350m to the
forestry gate where the Black Sail access track you have
been following meets the main forest road. Rather than
go through the gate onto the forest road veer right up the
pitched footpath by the side of a post-and-wire fence.

Pillar Rock dominates this end of the valley, overlooking the almost Alaskan blend of conifers and ice-
carved rock from its perch on the other side of the valley. ▸ The path continues to climb gently along the flank
of the fell, with the silver twists of the River Liza visible

Expect to see ravens,
buzzards and, if you
are fortunate, the
occasional peregrine
here.

far below. The fence-line you have been following runs out at a more substantial stream, which you follow upwards on the right-hand bank, ignoring the path to High Stile on its far bank. The going is good for the first few hundred metres, stone-pitched in places, but the path becomes less distinct near the top of **Scarth Gap pass**. When you reach the brow of the pass, seek out a well-used route to the left which descends into Buttermere valley.

The way down is something of a scramble, nothing technically difficult – just requiring care. In wet and misty weather the rocky pathway becomes one of an infinite number of watercourses, but thoughtfully placed cairns aid navigation. The path finally leaves the boulder field where it crosses a dry-stone wall, and soon becomes more distinct and easier underfoot as it moves into rough pasture and open fell, with the **Buttermere valley** unveiled beneath you.

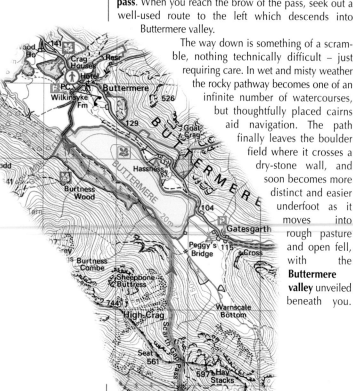

At a fenced enclosure of trees a crossroads in the path is reached. Go straight ahead for the lake shore rather than taking the right-hand path, which leads to Gatesgarth – unless you want to head this way for accommodation. Soon the main **lakeshore path** is reached; where this later forks, take either option. At the end of the lake go through the gate and over the two **footbridges** onto a wide gravel path that takes you along the edges of fields and into **Buttermere** village.

Descending Scarth Gap to Buttermere – the most direct route linking the Ennerdale and Buttermere valleys

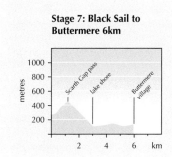

Stage 7: Black Sail to Buttermere 6km

Father and son taking a well-earned rest outside Black Sail hut

THE MAID OF BUTTERMERE

Buttermere was the scene for something of a national scandal back in 1802. In the years since, the sorry tale has evolved into a mixture of drama, legend and conjecture. The story was most recently brought to life as a novel by Cumbrian writer and broadcaster Melvyn Bragg.

The facts seem to be as follows. The story begins with one Mary Robinson, a noted local beauty and barmaid at Buttermere's Fish Inn. Possibly. Her charms attracted a visitor to the area, Colonel Hope MP, who arrived one day flush with money and aristocratic connections. He lost no time in trying to woo the young barmaid, and Mary, taken in by the man's charms, agreed to marry him.

However, on returning from their honeymoon (another tour of the Lakes!) Hope was unhappily revealed as both an imposter and a bigamist – much to Mary's distress. Curiously, the charge on which the imposter was arrested and tried was forgery – his letters were personally franked with his name as an MP – and on 3rd September 1803 a duly humbled Mr John Hatfield was hanged at Carlisle.

FURTHER EXPLORATION
Short Walk 6 is a two-hour excursion from Buttermere village to Scale Force, above nearby Crummock Water.

FACILITIES

Accommodation and food
For accommodation at **Black Sail** YH, see box at the end of Stage 6. The following are in or around **Buttermere** village.

Camping and B&Bs
The following three farms offer both camping spaces and rooms:
Syke Farm, tel: (017687) 70222
Simple campsite open Easter–October, right by the village
Dalegarth (+1½ miles; NY186160), tel: (017687) 70233
On the lake shore, southeast of the village
Gatesgarth Farm (+2 miles; NY195150), tel: (017687) 70256
Again, at the end of the lake

Youth hostel
Buttermere YH (+300m; NY179169), tel: (017687) 70245
Well-appointed hostel just outside the village, offering food also

Hotels
Fish Hotel, tel: (017687) 70253, and Bridge Hotel, tel: (017687) 70252
Two hotels, a stone's throw apart in the village, both offering rooms and bar food.

Transport
Buses leave from outside the cafe in the centre of the village. Between April and October there are regular services to Keswick via either Honister or Lorton.

STAGE 8
Buttermere to Keswick

Distance	9½ miles (15km)
Time	3½–4½hrs
Ascent	450m (1480ft)
Map	OS 1:25,000 OL4, Harvey Superwalker West sheet
Start point	Buttermere village, NY175069
Accommodation	Buttermere, Keswick
Refreshments	Pubs and tearooms in Buttermere and Portinscale

This is a satisfying and varied walk, starting in the quiet woodlands of Buttermere and heading towards the bustle of Keswick. Surprisingly, perhaps, considering the close proximity of Keswick, much of the stage is in solitude, with only the sound of tumbling waters and the cry of moorland birds for company. Few walkers venture along Sail and Rigg Becks – more usually this area is traversed by motor car along Newlands Hause further to the east. The stage concludes in the meadows of the Newlands valley, with walkers approaching Keswick via the village of Portinscale. There is little by way of refreshment until Portinscale (except a drink from a mountain stream perhaps). However, at Keswick, the end of the day, there is a wide choice of refreshment options – from cafes to pubs.

Opposite the **Bridge Hotel**, take the finger-posted path by Mill Beck, following its left bank through oak woodland. After 500m climb the ladder-stile over the wall on the left to leave the woodland and emerge onto open fell. Continue up the valley, keeping the wall immediately on your right. When the first wall ends 300m out of the woodland, ignore the footpath climbing up the hill and continue contouring at the same level, shortly following a second wall. After a few more minutes' walking, the second wall ends and becomes a post-and-wire fence. Continue along the path.

When you see a **sheepfold** on the other side of the beck, look out for a path heading up the hillside to the left. If you happen to miss this path and instead reach a stream with a dry-stone wall beyond, make your way upstream, where soon you will rejoin a more obvious path.

A HILL-FARMING YEAR

The Herdwick breed is synonymous with hill farming in the Lakeland fells. It is not now the only variety to be favoured by the area's farmers, but is still valued for its rugged, hardy characteristics – and its ability to spending much of its adult life high in the fell country.

In the Lakes, the hill-farming year starts with lambing in April, a little later than in the lowlands. Herdwicks have an uncanny ability to identity the small patch of fell of their early days as 'home'. When separated from this 'heaf', as it is known, for shearing or dipping, say, they will naturally tend to return to it. Thus on one hillside there may be several flocks of sheep, which may or may not belong to the same farmer, that will remain separate from each other.

Buttermere village, with not one – but two – pubs to choose from

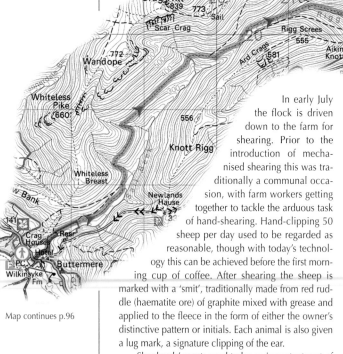

Map continues p.96

In early July the flock is driven down to the farm for shearing. Prior to the introduction of mechanised shearing this was traditionally a communal occasion, with farm workers getting together to tackle the arduous task of hand-shearing. Hand-clipping 50 sheep per day used to be regarded as reasonable, though with today's technology this can be achieved before the first morning cup of coffee. After shearing the sheep is marked with a 'smit', traditionally made from red ruddle (haematite ore) of graphite mixed with grease and applied to the fleece in the form of either the owner's distinctive pattern or initials. Each animal is also given a lug mark, a signature clipping of the ear.

Shepherds' meets used to be an important part of the hill-farming calendar, but now are more important simply as a social gathering. Traditionally they were the occasion for wayward sheep to be returned to their rightful owners and, in the autumn gatherings, for tups (rams) to be hired for the winter. The tups would then be put out with the ewes, and the ewes then 'dressed' with the red ruddle to indicate they had been serviced.

In the winter months the wethers (castrated rams) and ewes would be left out on the fells. The hoggs (younger sheep, yet to be shorn) would be overwintered off the fell, perhaps on nearby meadow land –

94

but at least with access to shelter. Nowadays the hoggs may be transported a considerable distance by road to fatten up on hay and sugar beet tops on lowland farms.

The path soon crosses an unnamed stream, beyond which the track climbs a little up the fell, then levels out on a well-defined path to **Third Gill**, where you again chase the waters uphill a little before crossing. Once over Third Gill, a fairly level 500m walk brings you to **Adacomb Beck**, and onto a well-defined path that meets **Rigg Beck**, which marks the start of the descent into Newlands valley.

As you follow Rigg Beck downstream, and turn a corner, Newlands valley comes into sight. As you reach the **Newlands road**, just to the left of a striking purple house, Rigg Beck disappears under a stone bridge. At the road, turn left and walk for 500m to **Rowling End Farm** to pick up a footpath to the right signed 'Ghyll Bank ½ mile'. Follow this to **Ghyll Bank** via a footbridge over Newlands Beck. At Ghyll Bank turn left along the minor road, taking care as there are blind corners. Ignore the footpath on the right, and continue towards Stair, about 600m from Ghyll Bank. Just beyond the **telephone box** you come to a T-junction. Take the right-hand turn to follow the road past the football grounds.

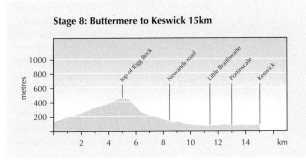

Stage 8: Buttermere to Keswick 15km

MINING IN THE NEWLANDS VALLEY

The name 'Newlands' refers to the land created by the Furness monks, who drained the former Husaker tarn and created valuable farmland on the rich soils. The name of the former tarn is echoed in today's Uzzicar Farm over to the left of the route. But it is mining rather than farming that Newlands is known for, with the long-lasting Goldscope mine (off your route, tucked into a southern corner of Newlands) providing the mainstay of the Keswick economy from Elizabethan times until

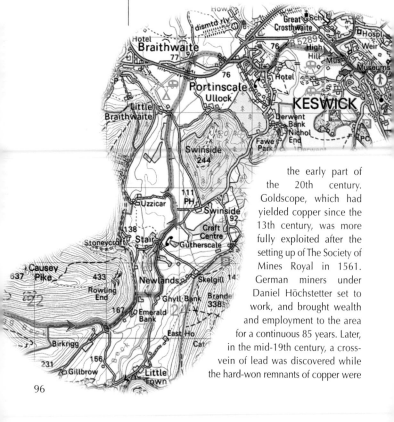

the early part of the 20th century. Goldscope, which had yielded copper since the 13th century, was more fully exploited after the setting up of The Society of Mines Royal in 1561. German miners under Daniel Höchstetter set to work, and brought wealth and employment to the area for a continuous 85 years. Later, in the mid-19th century, a cross-vein of lead was discovered while the hard-won remnants of copper were

On descending into Newlands, the first sign of habitation is the purple house

being extracted, and this gave the mine a second lease of life. Mining continued in a piecemeal fashion until its final demise after the First World War.

After the football grounds, a finger post indicating 'Little Braithwaite and Portinscale' leads over a stile to a foot-path through fields. As you walk through the meadows you pass a beautiful packhorse bridge to your left. ▶ At Little Braithwaite, cross over the road by the Weak Bridge and continue on through more fields, with the sound of the main Keswick road now present. After passing under this main road, head straight across the field to a gate by a smaller road and bridge. Turn left over the bridge, then right on a footpath signed with a finger post, and shortly pass through a gate marked 'footpath only'.

In early summer these meadows are ablaze with wild flowers.

*Sunset boats,
Derwentwater*

Refreshments:
Farmers Arms in
Portinscale is open
during the day, and
is walker- and
dog-friendly.

Following the footpath through fields, with Skiddaw to the left, head towards Keswick. The footpath joins a tarred lane for a few hundred metres until it meets the main road, which you cross over and follow the road opposite into **Portinscale**. ◄

In the centre of the village, turn left along the road passing **the Derwentwater Hotel**. When this road runs out, continue along the footpath and footbridge over the River Derwent, and through riverside fields to the town of **Keswick**. Follow the road into town, and you will find the tourist information centre at the Moot Hall in the market place – should you need it.

FACILITIES

Refreshments and accommodation
For accommodation in **Buttermere**, see box at end of Stage 7.

Keswick
Those seeking **hotel** or **B&B** accommodation are spoilt for choice in Keswick. Either take your chances on arrival, or contact Keswick TIC before arrival on (017687) 72645.

Camping
Campers need to head for the busy Derwentwater campsite (NY257235), tel: (017687) 72392, down by the lake, or alternatively head for the more simple site up at Castlerigg (+1 mile by footpath, NY282226 – see map).

Youth hostel
Keswick YH (NY268236), recently refurbished, is sited by the River Greta, just off Station Road, tel: (017687) 72484.

Transport
Buses leave Keswick from the bus stops by Lakes supermarket. From the Moot Hall head north along the main pedestrian area to the mini-roundabout by the Co-op and turn left for 100m. As well as frequent buses to Ambleside, Windermere and other destinations in the Lakes, a daily National Express service heads to London – slowly.

Market day in Keswick – amidst the outdoor shops are stalls selling local foods and crafts

STAGE 9
Keswick to Rosthwaite

Distance	8 miles (13km)
Time	2¾–3½hrs
Ascent	210m (690ft)
Maps	OS 1:25,000 OL4, Harvey Superwalker West sheet
Start point	Keswick Moot Hall, NY266234
Accommodation	Keswick, Grange, Rosthwaite
Refreshments	Keswick, Portinscale, Grange, Rosthwaite

Another short section, but one worth lingering over. Borrowdale, the setting for Stage 9, is arguably the most beautiful of the Lakeland valleys. Certainly, it was a favourite haunt of the 18th-century visitors arriving in search of the 'picturesque'. They would take in the framed views from the early tourist guide William Gilpin's carefully selected 'stations' around Derwentwater, chosen to include all the elements considered necessary for the picturesque – an awesome precipice, a mirror-smooth lake or serpentine river, and perhaps a lowly peasant or herd of cattle in the foreground.

The route starts out for Borrowdale from the market town of Keswick. The area has a long history. A little out of town, at Castlerigg, is one of the oldest Neolithic stone circles in Britain, predating Stonehenge by 1000 years. As for the town itself, the name Keswick (or rather 'Kesewic', meaning 'cheese farm') is first mentioned in a document of 1234, recording the sale of a farm to William of Derwentwater. In the early Middle Ages, Keswick rather languished in the shadow of rival market town Cockermouth, but in the reign of Queen Elizabeth I all this changed. Keswick found wealth in the hills, including copper from the Goldscope mine in Newlands, and later graphite from Borrowdale.

For all Keswick's industrial heritage, little of it is visible on the ground today. Borrowdale is the most lush of valleys, its rocky framework generously carpeted with every shade of deep green. Today the route passes through meadows and old woodlands, with Derwentwater and its islands forming the backdrop. There is minimal climbing, on an almost level route.

If you are not concerned about walking the entire Tour you could take the launch from Keswick to Hawes End, picking up the route description at this point. Between Easter and November, an hourly service connects the six jetties dotted about the lake. For details, tel: (017687) 72263, www.keswick-launch.co.uk.

Retrace your steps to **Portinscale**, picking up the signed path 'Portinscale ½ mile' opposite the Pencil Museum on the main road out of Keswick. This path starts out as a tarred lane, before turning right onto a very well-made gravel path. The bulk of Skiddaw dominates the view to the north; Whinlatter forest lies directly in front to the west, and the fells around Newlands just to the south-west. You're walking on a floodplain between the two lakes of Bassenthwaite and Derwentwater – coincidently this is the most northerly point of the Tour.

From the gravel path a kissing gate leads to a suspension **bridge** over the River Derwent and by a minor road into Portinscale. After passing the Derwentwater Hotel on the left, reach the T-junction in the road and turn left, walking down the road as far as **Nichol End** marina, passing another marina (Derwentwater) on the way. This section of the route is shared with both the Cumbria Way and the Allerdale Ramble. ▶

Leave the tarmac at Nichol End. Just past the entrance to the marina on the main road a footpath disappears into a gap in the hedge. Follow this footpath into the woodland, uphill. When the wooded path comes down on the far side of the knoll it meets a second path joining from the left. Ignore this and continue rightward for a few metres to a property named **Lingholm**. Here, you follow a footpath signed to Catbells, which continues between two lines of fencing through some delightful woodland – chestnut, beech and Scots pine to name but three species.

This section very much sets the scene for the day. You're still in the gentle scenery of the Skiddaw Slates, while further into Borrowdale, beyond Grange, the underlying geology of the Borrowdale Volcanic Group dictates a more rugged scenery. But here at Lingholm it's

Spotted orchid, photographed in Borrowdale in June

Refreshments:
If it is not too early in the day, Nichol End marina is not a bad place to stop for a coffee – you can sit overlooking the lake and its windsurfers and canoeists.

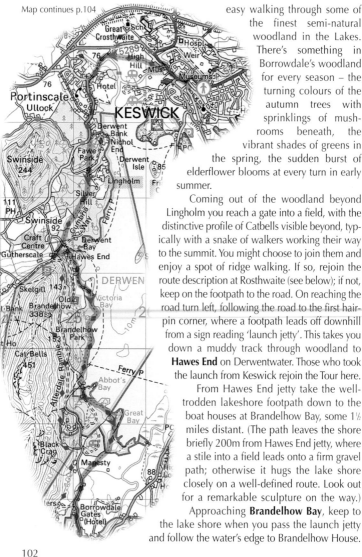

Map continues p.104

easy walking through some of the finest semi-natural woodland in the Lakes. There's something in Borrowdale's woodland for every season – the turning colours of the autumn trees with sprinklings of mushrooms beneath, the vibrant shades of greens in the spring, the sudden burst of elderflower blooms at every turn in early summer.

Coming out of the woodland beyond Lingholm you reach a gate into a field, with the distinctive profile of Catbells visible beyond, typically with a snake of walkers working their way to the summit. You might choose to join them and enjoy a spot of ridge walking. If so, rejoin the route description at Rosthwaite (see below); if not, keep on the footpath to the road. On reaching the road turn left, following the road to the first hairpin corner, where a footpath leads off downhill from a sign reading 'launch jetty'. This takes you down a muddy track through woodland to **Hawes End** on Derwentwater. Those who took the launch from Keswick rejoin the Tour here.

From Hawes End jetty take the well-trodden lakeshore footpath down to the boat houses at Brandelhow Bay, some 1½ miles distant. (The path leaves the shore briefly 200m from Hawes End jetty, where a stile into a field leads onto a firm gravel path; otherwise it hugs the lake shore closely on a well-defined route. Look out for a remarkable sculpture on the way.)

Approaching **Brandelhow Bay**, keep to the lake shore when you pass the launch jetty and follow the water's edge to Brandelhow House.

Borrowdale woodland in October, showing the russet colours typical of an autumn walk in the Lakes

From here, go through a field gate marked 'footpath' and follow the untarred road for 200m to a house called The Warren on the right. Here you turn left onto a footpath leading back to the lake shore. The route now meanders through lakeside woodlands and bracken on a well-maintained track, with gravelled and boardwalk sections, all the while with Derwentwater on the left. When you reach the end of the lake, look out for a path off to the right to Grange. Take this less obvious path rather than continuing around the head of the lake on the main path – which will dump you unhelpfully on the main Borrowdale road if you continue along it! The Grange path leads out to the quieter road near **Manesty**, where you turn left and continue into the village of Grange.

Grange is a pretty little village, its name harking back to its role as a storage and distribution centre in the years of the monasteries. Today it boasts a number of B&B establishments and two cafes, one with a riverside tea garden.

Leave the village by the side of Grange Cafe following signs for Hollins Farm. Keen-eyed geologists will spot the boundary between the Skiddaw Slates and the Borrowdale Volcanic series in this next section. After 500m, turn left off the main track into the campsite, following a rougher track with a dry-stone wall on the left and a wooded fell on the right. On clearing the campsite, the path reaches the riverside.

After crossing the footbridge over **Broadslack Gill** you are presented with a sign at a fork in the path with options

Stage 9: Keswick to Rosthwaite 13km

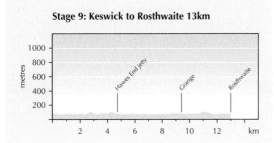

'Honister and Seathwaite' to the right and 'Rosthwaite' to the left. Keep left along a riverside path winding between the trees. When you reach a stone packhorse bridge over the River Derwent take this into **Rosthwaite**, unless you are heading for the youth hostel at Longthwaite, in which case stay on the western bank of the river to your destination.

Cottages in Stonethwaite, one of the best kept small Lakeland villages

FURTHER EXPLORATION

Short Walk 7 leaves Rosthwaite for a 2½hr circuit of the Borrowdale yew trees and the village of Seathwaite.

FACILITIES

Accommodation
For accommodation in **Keswick**, see box at end of Stage 8.

Grange
The Borrowdale Gates Hotel (NY251177), tel: (017687) 77204, and Hollows Farm B&B (NY247171), tel: (017687) 77298, are right on the route. For more possibilities, head on to Rosthwaite.

Rosthwaite

Camping
Chapel House Farm (+800m), tel: (017687) 77602. A basic site, just south of Rosthwaite (NY257140), by the road junction to Stonethwaite.
Stonethwaite Farm (+1 mile; NY268133), tel: (017687) 77234. Simple, riverside site. Also offers B&B accommodation at the farmhouse.

Youth hostel
Borrowdale YH (+500m; NY255143), tel: (017687) 77257, at Longthwaite
B&Bs and hotels
Yew Tree Farm, in the centre of the village by the Flock Inn cafe, tel: (017687) 77675
Two neighbouring hotels in the village offer beds and meals – the Royal Oak Hotel, tel: (017687) 77214, and the Scafell Hotel, tel: (017687) 77208.

Refreshments and supplies
Portinscale A cafe on main street; a second at Nichol End marina
Grange Two cafes, one with riverside tea garden
Rosthwaite Two pubs, one cafe and a post office with general store

Transport
The Borrowdale Rambler bus service connects Grange and Rosthwaite to Keswick. Services are frequent, with stops at numerous places along the B5289.

STAGE 10
Rosthwaite to Grasmere

Distance	7½ miles (12km)
Time	4½hrs
Ascent	605m (1990ft)
Maps	OS 1:25,000 OL 4,7; Harvey Superwalker West and Central sheets
Start point	Rosthwaite, NY259149
Accommodation	Rosthwaite, Stonethwaite, Grasmere
Refreshments	Rosthwaite (pubs and cafes), Stonethwaite (pub), Grasmere

Stage 10 leads away from the picture-postcard villages of Borrowdale to the valley's wilder recesses, and into scenery considered a little too rugged for the early tourists in Gilpin's wake. There is a change in flora too. The woodlands and orchid-filled meadows of the valley bottom are left behind on a climb up to the mosses above Grasmere, where tufts of cotton grass, sundews and bog asphodel punctuate these waterlogged uplands. Here there is a return to bird's-eye views – a retreating glimpse of lush Borrowdale and, over the watershed to Easedale, the sight of white water escaping its glacial tarn.

Journey's end is Grasmere, another charming if busy Lakeland village, well served with cafes, pubs and places to stay. Wordsworth fans may be tempted to linger here – there is plenty to explore.

Approaching **Rosthwaite**'s post office from the direction of the Flock Inn cafe, turn left on to the main Borrowdale road for 50m before turning right onto a bridleway signed 'Watendlath'. This old route from Rosthwaite to Watendlath marks the boundary between the two great agricultural estates of Furness Abbey and Fountains Abbey, and is a history lesson in itself – see section below.

FARMING THE LAND

The first farms of any significance in Borrowdale sprang up in the 10th century with the arrival of the Norsemen. Although there are signs of sporadic settlement by the Celtic and Roman people long before this, it was the Norsemen who undertook the daunting task of systematically clearing the land of boulders and forest to create viable farmland.

Later, under Norman occupation, farming grew to a much larger, commercial scale with vast areas of land under the control of the monastic estates. The Cistercian monks, who acquired their lands in Borrowdale from Lady Alice de Rumeli, ran an agrarian enterprise producing grains, wool and dairy products, all administered from monasteries in Furness and Yorkshire, and extracted taxes and tithes from the descendants of the Norse settlers.

From the late 12th century, the little village of Stonethwaite (then a dairy farm) was the centre of a rather unholy dispute between the two monasteries, which both claimed ownership. Eventually Edward I was consulted, who pragmatically decided the farm was in fact his and confiscated it from the monks – before selling it back to Fountains Abbey for 40 shillings!

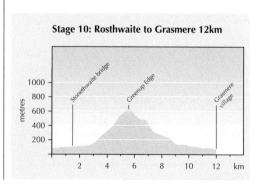

Stage 10: Rosthwaite to Grasmere 12km

Once over the bridge spanning Stonethwaite Beck follow the track right signed 'Stonethwaite 1 mile' along an old lonnin. Continue along the track until you reach **Stonethwaite Bridge**. ▶ There is also a simple

Stonethwaite village is well worth the short detour over this bridge, with its pretty cottages and quintessential Lakeland pub.

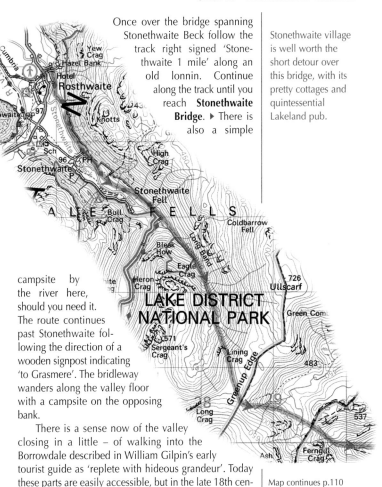

campsite by the river here, should you need it. The route continues past Stonethwaite following the direction of a wooden signpost indicating 'to Grasmere'. The bridleway wanders along the valley floor with a campsite on the opposing bank.

There is a sense now of the valley closing in a little – of walking into the Borrowdale described in William Gilpin's early tourist guide as 'replete with hideous grandeur'. Today these parts are easily accessible, but in the late 18th century these far reaches of Borrowdale beyond Rosthwaite – to Stonethwaite in the south, and Seathwaite to the south west – were almost inaccessible, cut off from the outside world by lack of roads, and had a 'Here be dragons' reputation.

Map continues p.110

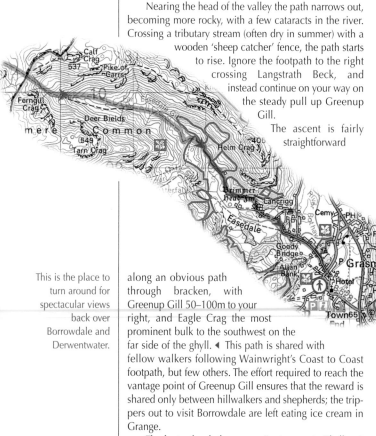

Nearing the head of the valley the path narrows out, becoming more rocky, with a few cataracts in the river. Crossing a tributary stream (often dry in summer) with a wooden 'sheep catcher' fence, the path starts to rise. Ignore the footpath to the right crossing Langstrath Beck, and instead continue on your way on the steady pull up Greenup Gill.

The ascent is fairly straightforward

This is the place to turn around for spectacular views back over Borrowdale and Derwentwater.

along an obvious path through bracken, with Greenup Gill 50–100m to your right, and Eagle Crag the most prominent bulk to the southwest on the far side of the ghyll. ◄ This path is shared with fellow walkers following Wainwright's Coast to Coast footpath, but few others. The effort required to reach the vantage point of Greenup Gill ensures that the reward is shared only between hillwalkers and shepherds; the trippers out to visit Borrowdale are left eating ice cream in Grange.

The footpath splashes across Footmoorgate Ghyll as it continues to climb, with the main Greenup Gill still to the right. It's a fair old climb, pleasant enough on a fair summer's day with a light pack and time on your side, but in poor weather or with a heavy pack it can be a real slog. As the path moves away from the shelter of the ghyll, the wind picks up and **Lining Crag** looms up close. Here take the path just to its left and continue on to the edge itself.

One short section of the climb up Lining Crag requires a little care over sometimes greasy rock before stone pitching completes the ascent. In case of mist, it may pay to take a compass bearing from the top of Lining Crag to Greenup Edge along the footpath, which is obvious enough on a clear day but may not be so in poor weather. It's a peaty morass of a trail, but with one or two small cairns to help you on your way.

When you reach the ridge line of **Greenup Edge**, NY286105 (which you will know by a line of aged iron posts marking the parish boundary), orientate your map using a compass to ensure that you take the path ahead (east) to Grasmere rather than Wythburn to the northeast or High Raise to the southwest. There's nothing more annoying than ending a hard day's hillwalking in the wrong valley, with an expensive taxi ride home!

The path dips a little to clip the top of the Wythburn valley before climbing a little again to the lip of **Far Easedale**. This part of the route is again a mixture of boulders and bog, followed by a mossy squelch to climb up to the ridgeline, once more adorned by iron posts, from which you gaze down into Far Easedale.

Drop into Far Easedale, following a footpath that will in time trace the course of the beck. In good weather, the distinctive profile of Helm Crag comes into view, and the white specks of the outlying buildings of

Cotton grass in June, Far Easedale – look out also for sundews at this time amidst the boggy ground

Walking up the Greenup Edge track – a backward glance back over Borrowdale

Accommodation:
There are three
hostels in Grasmere.
For YHA's Thorney
Howe turn off at the
first side road on the
left; otherwise
continue into the
village.

Grasmere. At **Stythwaite Steps** cross a footbridge to the other side of the beck. When the path reaches the valley floor it becomes a more obvious track, between two dry-stone walls, passing some outlying buildings on the left. Turn round to catch the milky waters of Sourmilk Gill in the distance to the northwest.

Keep on along the walled track, through some houses at **Lancrigg**, until you reach the tarred road, then turn left into the **Grasmere**. ◄

FURTHER EXPLORATION

Short Walk 8 is a scenic half-day walk from Grasmere with a Wordsworth theme.

FACILITIES

Accommodation

For accommodation in **Rosthwaite** and **Stonethwaite** see the box at the end of Stage 9.

Grasmere

Youth hostels

Grasmere has two youth hostels in the YHA network – the smaller Thorney Howe (NY332084)is a former farmhouse 200m off the route, and Butterlyp Howe (NY337079) is a large Victorian villa close to the town centre. Both can be contacted on tel: (015394) 35316.

Grasmere's Independent Hostel, tel: (015394) 35055, is *en route*, a little out of the village just north of Mill Bridge on the A591, 20 minutes' walk into Stage 11. For bookings, tel: (015394) 35055.

B&Bs and hotels

There are a large number of places to stay in Grasmere, but the village also gets a very large number of visitors – booking ahead is advised. The National Park Information Centre on (015394) 35245 may be able to help, if the suggestions below draw a blank. Note that many establishments in Grasmere impose a two- night minimum stay, especially at weekends.

Harwood in Red Lion Square, tel: (015394) 35248, and How Beck on Broadgate, tel: (015394) 35732, are two modestly priced, family-run establishments. A little out of town, but handy for Dove Cottage, is How Foot

Lodge, tel: (015394) 35366. Well-heeled vegetarians will appreciate Lancrigg (NY328085), which is passed on the way into Grasmere in Easedale, tel: (015394) 35317.

For hotels, there's the Red Lion in the heart of the village, tel: (015394) 35456, and the Wordsworth Hotel (NY341069), tel: (015394) 35592 – Grasmere's finest, overlooking the lake near Dove Cottage. The Swan Hotel (NY340083), tel: (015394) 35551, is on the main road, but well sited for an early start on Stage 11.

Refreshments and supplies

Stonethwaite	The Langstrath Inn (+200m; NY264137) for bar food, beer garden
Grasmere	Numerous cafes, pubs and restaurants
	Post office / general store
	Outdoor equipment shops

Transport

Grasmere is on the 555 bus route from Kendal to Keswick. Change at Ambleside for Coniston and Langdale; Keswick for Borrowdale or Buttermere; and Windermere for the infrequent service to Patterdale.

Far Easedale walls and ruins – many of the valleys visited along the way have long abandoned structures such as this

STAGE 11
Grasmere to Patterdale

Distance	7¾ miles (12.5km)
Time	3½–4hrs
Ascent	635m (1810ft)
Map	OS 1:25,000 OL5, OL7; Harvey Superwalker Central sheet
Start point	Grasmere, NY337076
Accommodation	Grasmere, Patterdale (+1 mile)
Refreshments	Grasmere, Patterdale
High-level alternative	Grasmere to Patterdale via Helvellyn and Swirral Edge (see Part 3, High Level 4)

For many Grasmere is synonymous with the poet Wordsworth, who with his sister Dorothy made Dove Cottage his home for the most productive nine years of his life. During his time here his reputation as a poet grew, and the village became as famous as the poet himself. It was of course the landscape that inspired Wordsworth, and there is much landscape to take in. The Tour merely touches Grasmere village, before heading once more to the hills above. If time permits, a stop-over day here is well worthwhile – the short walk 'Wordsworth's Grasmere and Rydal', described later in this book (Part 4, Walk 8), explores the surroundings of the valley a little more thoroughly.

This stage of the walk heads quickly away from the hubbub of the village, escaping along a side road and up towards Helvellyn (to go via Helvellyn, take the alternative high-level route). It's a day out in the wilds, with efforts rewarded by views of some of England's highest peaks. Stock up on food and drink before leaving Grasmere, as there is nothing until you reach the Patterdale Hotel at the end of the stage.

Locate the bookshop in the centre of **Grasmere**, and head out on the Easedale road immediately opposite, passing Butterlyp Howe YH 100m along the way. After a further 500m take the unnamed road to the right, signed to Thorney Howe Youth Hostel. Pass the entrance to this second hostel, keeping on the lane heading to the main Grasmere to Keswick road in the distance. The lane heads down and over a packhorse bridge to join the main road 200m up from the **Traveller's Rest** pub.

Map continues p.116

Cross the main road to follow the bridleway opposite, to Patterdale. The way starts as a quiet lane passing through some houses, ascending steadily on a cobbled track amidst bracken, with Tongue Gill bubbling away 100m or so below. Approaching the spur of a hill ahead known as the **Great Tongue**, go through a field gate, and the path narrows and veers leftward away from the gill. Cross over the tributary to the left. A footbridge is provided to take you over the tributary should the waters be in spate. Now chase the tributary just crossed uphill, to the **left** of the Great Tongue.

Head for the most prominent crags under **Seat Sandal**. The path becomes less distinct as you get within about 400m of the crags, but pick your way up carefully, and pass along the top of the crags to head back toward Tongue Gill and the top of the valley. Leg muscles are given a brief reprieve on a section of level then undulating ground on a well-trodden path, partly cairned. A final uphill push ends at **Grisedale Hause**, the highest point of today's walk. At the Hause is a dramatic vantage point – Grisedale Tarn sits below you, with Dollywagon Pike behind, Seat Sandal to your left, and the St Sunday Crag path leading off to your right. ▶

On a fine day it might well be tempting to take the high-level alternative up Dollywagon and on to Helvellyn (see Part 3, High Level 4).

The route then heads down to **Grisedale Tarn**. This is a terrific spot for a wild camp, nestled between the high fells. If your schedule allows, it is worth trying to time your walk to arrive at the tarn late in the day – the still waters perfectly catch the evening light. At the end of the tarn splash through the out-flowing beck to take the path heading under the crags of Dollywagon Pike. Once under the crags the path levels out briefly before commencing its winding descent to Patterdale. Pass the Outward Bound bothy **of Ruthwaite Lodge**, keeping on the right-hand side of the beck – ignore a tempting plank footbridge. A little further on, 500m from the lodge, **do** go over a second footbridge spanning a beck coming down from St Sunday Crag.

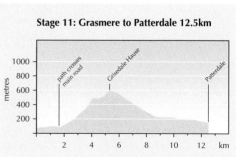

Stage 11: Grasmere to Patterdale 12.5km

The way from Grasmere initially follows this quiet tarred lane, before crossing the main road to a bridleway

As the path reaches the valley floor, it widens out into a farm track, becoming tarred ½ mile out of Patterdale. On the tarred section, on coming to a field gate across the track keep straight on. At a left-hand bend in the road take a signed footpath to the right past some farm buildings. Go through a gate into a field on the left, to walk over a grassy hillock and over a wall stile at the far end of the field. Once over the stile, turn left and head downhill through the birch trees to the village of **Patterdale**.

FURTHER EXPLORATION

Short Walk 9 (actually a walk plus steamer ride) is a great half-day outing for walkers of all abilities.

Heading up toward Grisedale Tarn on the path via Tongue Gill

Post Office, Patterdale village

FACILITIES

Accommodation
For accommodation in **Grasmere**, see box at the end of Stage 10.
Accommodation is very limited in **Patterdale**.

Youth hostel and camping
Patterdale YH (+300m; NY399157) is on the main Kirkstone road, tel:
(017684) 82394.
The small Side Farm campsite (+500m; NY398163), beautifully sited at the
head of Ullswater, offers simple but clean facilities with showers, tel:
(017687) 82338.

Hotels and B&Bs
The Ullswater View guesthouse, tel: (017687) 82175, on the road just south
of the village centre, has rooms. The White Lion pub, tel: (017687) 82214,
also has a few rooms available, or try the large Patterdale Hotel, tel: (017687)
82231.

Refreshments and supplies
Grasmere   Various pubs, cafes, post office, Co-op, gear shops
Patterdale   One pub, one hotel, post office and general store

Transport
Patterdale is very poorly served with public transport. See the Transport section in the Introduction.

119

STAGE 12
Patterdale to Windermere

Distance	13 miles (21km)
Time	5½–7hrs
Ascent	2490ft (760m)
Maps	OS 1:25,000 OL5, OL7, Harvey Superwalker East and Central sheets
Start point	Patterdale, NY397159
Accommodation	Patterdale, Windermere
Refreshments	Patterdale village, Troutbeck (+1 mile), Windermere
High-level alternative	Patterdale to Windermere via High Street (see Part 3, High Level 5)

So this is it – the last stage of the Tour. Congratulations if you have made it this far! This final section is a suitable finale – a full day in the hills, bringing you slowly back to civilisation. This route is recommended in preference to the high-level alternative if weather conditions are poor, as wayfinding is more secure on this lower-level route. Stock up on food and water in Patterdale before setting out, and expect to be on the fells for most of the day, with just ravens, buzzards and deer for company.

Patterdale, our starting point, is a compact collection of houses clustered around the road on the Ullswater side of the Kirkstone Pass. Its one pub, the White Lion, has long been a port of call for travellers heading north from the central Lakes. Mining and the wool trade have provided an income to Patterdale and neighbouring Glenridding through the ages. The area is littered with evidence of past efforts to extract copper, lead and slate – most notably at Greenside, once the world's second largest lead mine, in the Glenridding valley. A curious spin-off for sleepy Patterdale was that its school and church were amongst the first in the country to get electricity, powered by an early hydro-electric scheme at the mine.

From the **Patterdale Hotel**, leave the village heading in the Kirkstone Pass direction. Take the 'no through road' to the left, 200m from the post office. This enticing lane leads to a group of houses, where you turn right along

Crookabeck Houses, tucked away on a quiet lane on the way to Hartsop

another lane signed 'Footpath Hartsop'. Keeping on the main track go through the houses at **Crookabeck**, one with a delightfully carved wooden fence surrounding a vegetable garden. Go through a field gate at the far end of the property marked 'footpath only' that leads into ash woodland colonised by grey squirrels.

Some 600m from Crookabeck, the track reaches another farmstead named **Beckstones**. Again, keep on the main track, passing through a field gate to reach a hairpin bend in the track. At the hairpin, go left (uphill) on the bridleway signed 'Hartsop', rather than taking the bridleway down to Deepdale Bridge. On reaching some waterfalls 500m from the hairpin, you will see a ladder-stile going over a wall. Ignore this – instead take the small wooden footbridge lower down leading into a gated lonnin.

The bridleway leads past the wooden chalets of Hartsop Fold, after which the lane becomes tarred. To the left of the bridleway you will see the buildings of Crossgatesgill Farm, and beyond are the moody Angle Pikes, which have been marking your progress this morning. Now ahead of you is the more benign Hartsop Dodd, and you head in this direction, continuing on the bridleway.

The first sign of **Hartsop** village itself is the bright red of the telephone box coming into view. Turn left at Langton Venture Centre to enter the village, ignoring the footpath off to the right a few metres after the venture centre. Keep on climbing gently through this very pictur-esque village as the main thoroughfare turns into a bridle-way and is joined by a footpath leading in from the left.

HARTSOP VILLAGE

Now a peaceful village, set away from today's main road, in the past Hartsop had a bigger population than either Glenridding or Patterdale. In medieval times it became an important wool-spinning town, supplying cloth to Kendal by packhorses over the Kirkstone Pass. The village has also been quite a centre of mining

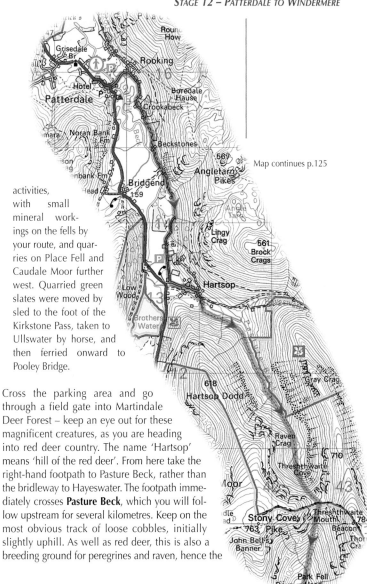

Map continues p.125

activities, with small mineral workings on the fells by your route, and quarries on Place Fell and Caudale Moor further west. Quarried green slates were moved by sled to the foot of the Kirkstone Pass, taken to Ullswater by horse, and then ferried onward to Pooley Bridge.

Cross the parking area and go through a field gate into Martindale Deer Forest – keep an eye out for these magnificent creatures, as you are heading into red deer country. The name 'Hartsop' means 'hill of the red deer'. From here take the right-hand footpath to Pasture Beck, rather than the bridleway to Hayeswater. The footpath immediately crosses **Pasture Beck**, which you will follow upstream for several kilometres. Keep on the most obvious track of loose cobbles, initially slightly uphill. As well as red deer, this is also a breeding ground for peregrines and raven, hence the

On the footpath from Hartsop by Pasture Beck, a fine example of the art of dry-stone walling – here a sheepfold

notices prohibiting climbing on the aptly named Raven Crag until the end of the breeding season. The route later leads past Raven Crag, so follow the signs to Raven Crag through a field gate with a ladder-stile to the side, whereupon the path swings round to the left by a wall. All this within 200m of the car park!

The path is a little way from Pasture Beck at this point, but comes in closer further up. On the far side of the beck are some old mine workings and settling tanks, and dotted about the hillside beyond are signs of abandoned levels, relics of Hartsop's mining history. Hartsop

Stage 12: Patterdale to Windermere 21km

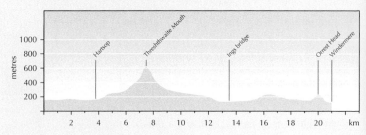

Dodd is now to your right. Go over a ladder-stile by a gate to continue chasing the beck up to the top of the valley, with the path now almost at the beck side.

At the drumlins under Raven Crag the path leaves the valley floor and starts zigzagging its way up to a pass known as Threshthwaite Mouth. A short section of stone pitching leads close to the bottom of **Raven Crag**, and this is a good vantage point to turn round and look back towards Hartsop. Almost opposite Raven Crag, by the beck, is a well-preserved sheep-fold. Once beyond Raven Crag a clear, part-pitched path leads most of the way to the top of the pass. The very last few metres to the top at **Threshthwaite Mouth** may be indistinct in mist – look out for cairns to guide you. Suddenly, you reach a dry-stone wall and – bang – Troutbeck valley and Windermere appear under your feet. Straddle atop a boulder on Threshthwaite Mouth and you can see Windermere with the left eye and Ullswater with the right.

The path down into the Troutbeck valley from the Mouth is rather less obvious, but you are unlikely to go far wrong. Start your descent from the Stony Cove Pike end of the pass, and make your way down the grassy slope, later keeping to the right of the beck as you go down. The going is a bit squelchy in places – in particularly dire spots try to pick a route with stepping stones to save being consumed by the mire. As you

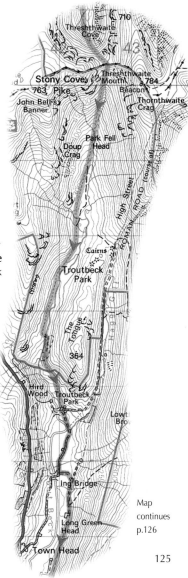

Map
continues
p.126

come across any tributary streams joining from the right, cross over them and stay on the right-hand side of the main beck.

On reaching the outlying dry-stone wall of the valley, go through a gate in the wall to some derelict sheepfolds, engulfed in the bracken. The path is indistinct from the sheepfolds, but a route slightly higher up the hillside to the right will avoid the worst of the morass, leading into a difficult-to-spot path through the bracken. Splash through a stream and clamber over a bracken-covered knoll to reach a second dry-stone wall with a single wooden gate in it. You are heading for The Tongue, the hill marooned in the base of the Troutbeck valley, just ahead.

Go through the gate to see **The Tongue** now on the left. How distinct the path is from here (as with many others) will depend on the time of year; in summer it may be obscured by bracken. As you come down the valley, past The Tongue, look out for a **bridge** constructed with stone flags, wide enough (if not strong enough) to take a vehicle. Take this bridge to pick up a footpath by the river bank leading around the base of The Tongue. Here by the beck are some beautiful places to paddle weary feet on a hot summer's day, or to admire the splashing meltwaters at a respectful distance in February! At the bottom of The

Troutbeck valley, formerly a royal hunting forest, leads back towards Windermere

Tongue the path veers away from the beck, heading through a field gate in the wall to descend via a rocky path to a farm at **Troutbeck Park**. As you approach the farm, head to the right of the buildings, then left in front of the farm onto a gravel track on the valley floor.

In summer the verges of the road south from the farm at Troutbeck Park are ablaze with stitchwort, herb Robert, buttercups, meadow cranesbill and speedwells. On older maps of the Lake District this is marked as an un-metalled road, but in fact it has changed – tarmac has reached this and many other outlying Lakeland farms in recent years. Just before **Ing Bridge** take the road turning to the left, with a hand-written sign saying 'Long Green Head': this brings you out after 250m onto the High Street track. Turn right and follow it down the valley, to the left of the buildings at **Long Greenhead** Farm.

The bridleway continues past the farm. At a fork in the track **above Limefitt caravan park**, keep left and slightly uphill. After a field gate the track merges with the Garburn Pass trail coming in from the left. Very shortly afterwards the path ahead forks – take the left-hand option, slightly uphill. Keep on the track until you reach the Troutbeck–Ings road at a **T-junction**. Great views of Windermere are now revealed ahead.

At this T-junction, turn right to head downhill for 200m, before picking up the footpath to Far Orrest on

National Trust farm at Troutbeck Park – many of the old Lakeland farms are in the ownership of the National Trust and run by tenant farmers

the left side of the road. Follow the footpath, in time coming to a field gate leading into a lonnin to Far Orrest. Instead of crossing the farm at **Far Orrest**, take the footpath just before it to the left. This heads to Near Orrest, clipping the edge of the field before going through two sets of kissing gates guarding another lonnin.

From the kissing gates go through a field and over a ladder-stile, then through a second field and over a second stile. Continue through two similar fields to a kissing gate before **Near Orrest Farm**. Here head to another kissing gate to the right of the farm, where the path emerges onto a tarred lane. Turn right to follow the lane for 200m before picking up a footpath to the left to Orrest Head and Windermere. Choose a path leading to the top for a last well-earned pause at the **Orrest Head** viewpoint, before saying your farewells to the fells and heading downhill at the far side. The path will lead you back to your starting point, **Windermere** railway station.

FACILITIES

Accommodation and transport
See Stage 1.

PART 3
HIGH-LEVEL
ALTERNATIVE ROUTES

*The path from Low Water
leading up to the summit of
Coniston Old Man (High Level 1)*

HIGH LEVEL 1
*Coniston to Eskdale via
the Old Man and Hardknott*

Distance	11 miles (17.5km)
Time	5–7½hrs
Total ascent	1050m (3440ft)
Maps	OS 1:25,000 OL6, Harvey Superwalker South West sheet
Start point	Coniston village, SO303976
Accommodation	Coniston, Eskdale
Refreshments	Coniston village; Woolpack Inn, Eskdale

This high-level route is an alternative to the main route Stage 4.

At 803m (2635ft) the Old Man may not be Lakeland's tallest peak (indeed it doesn't even make the top 10) but it is certainly one of the most loved and visited in the central fells. Towering over the little town of Coniston, this benevolent patriarch has shared its wealth of copper and slate over the centuries, and wears its scars of past mining enterprise with dignity and pride. Every year, thousands of visitors make the two-hour ascent from the village for pleasure – one can only marvel at the stamina of the miners of yesteryear who made their way up merely to start a hard day's work!

As a mountain walk, an ascent of the Old Man has all the right ingredients – an interesting approach along Coppermines valley to set the scene, a climb up to Low Water (pause for breath), then a final push for the summit. It's like a Himalayan peak in miniature, as any fan of Arthur Ransome's children's books will surely know.

If the first part of this walk is familiar and well trodden, the second part is perhaps much less so. At Goat's Hause the crowds and boot-smoothed footpaths are left behind, and the descent to Seathwaite Tarn may well be enjoyed in solitude. Your destination for the day is approached via the quiet upper reaches of the Duddon valley, before a majestic entrance to Eskdale is made above the Roman fort at Hardknott. The route chosen is challenging but achievable for the averagely fit walker, and is a good way to test your mountain legs before committing to the high-level alternatives in later days. Note, the route requires crossing the Duddon by stepping stones – if the waters are likely to be unusually high, a deviation will be necessary.

Tempting though it was to include other peaks whilst 'high' on the fells – Wetherlam, Swirl How and Harter Fell perhaps – 11 miles and over 1000m (3500ft) of ascent is likely to be enough for most at this stage in a long-distance walk. At least it was for me. You might, however, like to consider a combination of this and the low-level route – Coniston Old Man then on to Dow Crag, Brown Pike and the Walna Scar road, for example. I leave it up to you to decide.

Leave the hubbub of Coniston from the little bridge by Barclays Bank, taking the small lane by the offices of Coniston Coppermines Cottages – you will see a sign pointing to the Sun Inn. The lane climbs up to the white-washed 16th-century inn, behind which you will find a public footpath signed to 'Old Man and Levers Water'. Follow the right of way along the tarred lane beyond the last of the houses to a small gate leading onto a farm track. Here you will be greeted by the sound of Church Beck, crashing its way toward the lake.

Coniston Coppermines Youth Hostel, a former mine-worker's cottage, in a lonely spot high above Coniston

Ignore the footbridge leading over Church Beck away to your right, but keep on upwards on the farm track on the left-hand side of the beck. Some 500m upstream from the footbridge you will come to the most spectacular of the falls, under the packhorse-style **Miner's Bridge**. Again, don't cross over the bridge, but

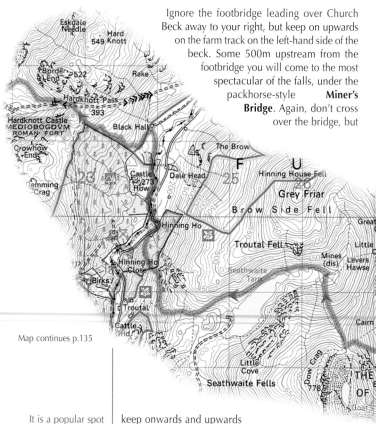

Map continues p.135

It is a popular spot for ghyll scrambling here – you may see brightly clad and helmeted youngsters being guided up the less precipitous sections of the falls.

keep onwards and upwards on the near bank. ◄

Beyond Miner's Bridge the path starts to lead away from the beckside. **Coppermines Youth Hostel**, with its bracken-coloured spoil heaps, now occupies centre frame across the valley. Beyond and to the right of the hostel, above the waterfalls and mine workings, the peak of Wetherlam is visible. To the left of the Coppermines hostel, above the waterfalls leaving Levers Water, you may make out the distinctive profile of Swirl How.

ARTHUR RANSOME AND CONISTON

In 1903, the eminent writer and antiquarian W. G. Collingwood was making his way down Church Beck after a day's sketching in the mountains. Seeing an immobile body on a rock by the beck he enquired, 'Young man ... are you alive?' The body was that of the then 17-year-old Arthur Ransome, dozing after an afternoon composing poetry. The chance encounter between the teenage writer and the encouraging older intellectual marked the start of a lifetime link between Ransome, the Collingwood family and Coniston. The young Ransome, in awe of the author of *Thorstein of the Mere*, shared the older man's passion for the lake country and became a regular visitor to the Collingwood household.

In later life, following his work as the *Manchester Guardian's* Russian correspondent, Ransome came back to the Coniston area to

settle – and write his most famous works, including *Swallows and Amazons*. Ransome drew on the younger Collingwoods as models for the fictional characters in his children's books, and on the geography of the Coniston area for his backdrop. To the generations of readers enjoying Ransome's work since publication in the 1930s

High Level 1: Coniston to Eskdale via Old Man and Hardknott 17.5km

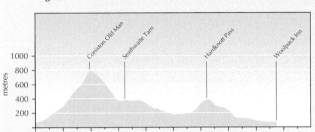

Lake Coniston from Old Man path – on cloudy days the best views are sometimes had before hitting the summit itself

Coniston holds a curious place in the imagination: the Old Man grows in the mind to Kanchenjunga; the steam yacht *Gondola* into Captain Flint's houseboat. One cannot but wonder whether these stories would have been left untold had it not been for the meeting by Church Beck.

On your side of the valley, roughly level with the Coppermines hostel, the path now goes through two out-lying stone walls, then climbs steadily leftwards, leaving views of the Coppermines valley behind. Where the path leads up to a junction with a track, turn right, and continue to follow the slate track as it zigzags upwards, more steeply now, into the crags and old mine workings.

You now climb up into the old mining area – adorned with rusty hawsers, long abandoned machinery and mysterious entrance holes into the old levels. The height gained earns views back over Coniston lake and village. Keep on the main path as it picks its way upwards through the loose spoil to reach the turquoise-green **Low Water**. Low Water marks the start of the final push to the summit, straightforward but steep. The path is littered with boulders, and is stone pitched in places.

When you reach the summit of the **Old Man**, on a clear day it will provide a 360º vista of the hills of the South Lakes – Dow Crag, Brown Pike and Wetherlam nearest to hand, with the Langdale Pikes a little further away to the north. To the east lie the valleys of Coniston and Windermere, which you leave behind at this point. Further afield, to the south

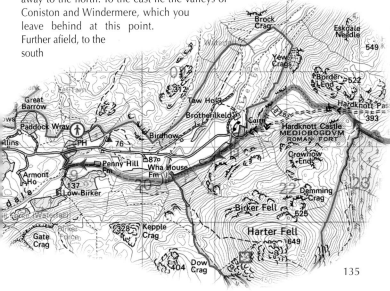

The path from Low Water leading up to the summit of Coniston Old Man

and west, you can see the outline of Morecambe Bay and the west Cumbrian coast.

To continue from the summit, head northwards initially for 400m along the ridge, until a cairn marks the start of a path heading left down to Goat's Hause, the pass between the summits of the Old Man and Dow Crag. After reaching **Goat's Hause**, follow the beck down Far Gill in a northwesterly direction.

For much of the descent down the gill there is not a clear path, as it's little used. Just keep to the right of the beck, following it down to the valley floor and a sheepfold. Once at the valley floor, cross over the becks where convenient, and negotiate the marshy ground to more solid footings on the northerly side. Now head left toward Seathwaite Tarn, taking a route just under the crags on the valley floor. Approaching the weir at **Seathwaite Tarn**, head right, and contour round the crags. Keep between the beck on your left and the crags on your right. Ignore a discreetly signed footpath off to the left under the crags 'To Duddon Valley', keeping straight ahead. Shortly you will get to the lip of the valley, from where you descend to a dry-stone wall, with Dunnerdale opening up beneath you.

The path continues through a gap in the wall. Here you turn right and follow the wall as it contours around the base of the crags. The path is not always distinct, so use the wall as a wayfinder. Where the wall runs into a large outcrop in a corner, follow it the 50m or so downhill to the entrance to the **plantation** ahead – a gap in the wall leads to a wooden stile taking you into the trees. An easy-to-follow footpath leads through the conifers to the other side.

When out of the woodland, follow the signed footpath rightwards to join the small road visible below. Continue northwards along the road, passing **Hinning House**. As the road meets the River Duddon, 200m from Hinning House, some **stepping stones** lead across the river. Take these if it is safe to do so. If the waters are too high, continue along the road to the next house, **Dale Head**. Here a public footpath off to the left takes you to a second set of stepping stones. Either way, turn right after crossing the river to follow the bankside bridleway to Black Hall Farm.

At the farmyard gate at **Black Hall** take the footpath off to the left, which climbs the slope and ultimately joins the road at the top of the Hardknott Pass. This last bit of climbing for the day (200m of ascent over 1500m) is not too arduous. From Black Hall Farm the tractor track heads up to the plantation on the fellside, from where the footpath zigzags up the fell by the edge of the trees. At the top corner of the plantation, veer right, heading over the stile and continuing on a path to the Hardknott road.

Follow the road down, past **Hardknott Roman fort**, to the cattle grid at the foot of the pass. The verges at the side of the road make for a more comfortable hike downhill – or as comfortable as serious downhill can be at the end of the day. With good luck and clear weather, you may be able to see all the way down the valley of the Esk to the sea, with the Isle of Man beyond.

HARDKNOTT FORT

The windswept stronghold of Hardknott (Mediobocdum) provided the link from Roman Ravenglass to Ambleside. Mediobocdum would have been a full-scale defensive fort, with walls 12 feet thick – a little more substantial than would be needed simply to keep the rain out! The complex included barracking, bath houses and granaries, with a lot still discernable today. Just by the side of the road, you can explore the site at will or simply admire the views and rest weary feet before the descent into Eskdale.

From the cattle grid, take the tiny **Jubilee bridge** over the beck to the left and pick up the footpath beyond, through a pair of kissing gates. Now head down to the wall on the right and follow it along, ignoring a larger track heading uphill to your left. At the end of this first field go through another kissing gate and continue along the easy-to-follow path for the mile to **Penny Hill Farm**.

At Penny Hill Farm, a permitted path skirts round the farmyard to join a lane leading to Doctor Bridge. Cross over **Doctor Bridge**, turn right and continue to the main road. For the **Woolpack Inn** in Eskdale, head right along the road for 200m.

FACILITIES

Accommodation and transport
See Stage 4 on the main route.

HIGH LEVEL 2
Eskdale to Wasdale Head
via Scafell Pike

Distance	10 miles (16.5km)
Time	5–7hrs
Total ascent	1065m (3500ft)
Maps	OS 1:25,000 OL6, Harvey Superwalker West sheet
Start point	Woolpack Inn, NY190010
Accommodation	Wasdale Head – campsite and inn only
Refreshments	Wasdale Head Inn

This high-level route is an alternative to the main route Stage 5.

A great advantage of a multi-day walk is the freedom to walk in one direction, without having to circle back to a car or base at the end. This route over Scafell Pike really makes the most of this opportunity. England's highest peak is savoured, as perhaps it should be – first, a lengthy and respectful approach to the base of the mountain, with the final push to the summit left until the second half of the day. Scafell Pike is most commonly tackled as a round trip from Wasdale, this being the closest point of civilisation, but your route leaves the short stone-pitched tourist route for the descent, and makes its approach via the rugged, unspoilt beauty of upper Eskdale. It follows the languid curves of the River Esk up almost to its source under Esk Pike, before making for the col between Broad Crag and Scafell Pike, via Little Narrowcove Beck.

Stock up well before leaving the Eskdale valley, as there's nothing by way of supplies or refreshment until Wasdale Head. But then, the away-from-it-all feel is very much the appeal of this particular route.

In **Eskdale**, whether you have been staying at the Woolpack Inn or in the village of Boot, retrace your steps from yesterday to the Penny Hill Farm sign on the main road, and take the no-through road to **Doctor Bridge**. Head over the bridge and left along the lane to pick up the permitted path to the right, avoiding the farm itself.

Continue along the signposted valley-floor path to the **cattle grid** at the bottom of Hardknott Pass, one mile distant. It is an easy path to follow, the only point to note is where your path meets a bridleway sign pointing left to Wha House Bridge. Ignore this option and continue straight ahead.

From the cattle grid, head down the road a little to the red phone box, tucked away on the right-hand side of the road – presumably for motorists to report cars expiring on the journey over from Langdale! Here, pick up the right of way following the farm track to **Brotherilkeld Farm**. Pass the farm to the left as the signs direct, following the beck. Ignore an early option to take a footbridge to Scafell Pike and Taw House, and continue ahead into the fields.

As you pass through the three fields beyond Brotherilkeld Farm, you will see the falls of Scale Gill over to your left. Leave the last field by the ladder-stile over the boundary wall, from where the path leads back down towards the river again. There are at least two paths heading this way, and which you take is unimportant – both converge by the river a little below Lingcove Bridge.

Here in Upper Eskdale there are several hours of wonderful walking through an upland wilderness,

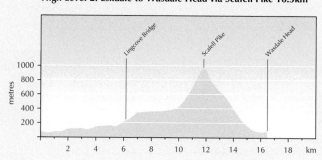

High Level 2: Eskdale to Wasdale Head via Scafell Pike 16.5km

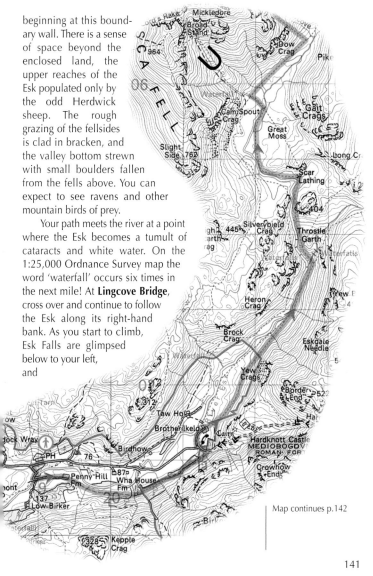

beginning at this boundary wall. There is a sense of space beyond the enclosed land, the upper reaches of the Esk populated only by the odd Herdwick sheep. The rough grazing of the fellsides is clad in bracken, and the valley bottom strewn with small boulders fallen from the fells above. You can expect to see ravens and other mountain birds of prey.

Your path meets the river at a point where the Esk becomes a tumult of cataracts and white water. On the 1:25,000 Ordnance Survey map the word 'waterfall' occurs six times in the next mile! At **Lingcove Bridge**, cross over and continue to follow the Esk along its right-hand bank. As you start to climb, Esk Falls are glimpsed below to your left, and

Map continues p.142

141

immediately ahead lies the bulk of **Throstlehow Crag**. Pass the crag to the left by the river. The river bends sharply 300m beyond the crag – negotiate the boggy ground to follow the river leftward under **Scar Lathing**.

Now as you head northwest, the milk-white streaks of the water falling from **Cam Spout** are clearly seen ahead. Follow the river along its

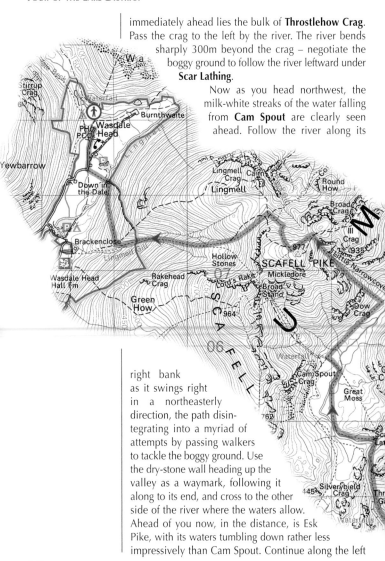

right bank as it swings right in a northeasterly direction, the path disintegrating into a myriad of attempts by passing walkers to tackle the boggy ground. Use the dry-stone wall heading up the valley as a waymark, following it along to its end, and cross to the other side of the river where the waters allow. Ahead of you now, in the distance, is Esk Pike, with its waters tumbling down rather less impressively than Cam Spout. Continue along the left

Quiet Upper Eskdale on the route to Scafell Pike, a rewarding and interesting approach to England's highest mountain

bank of the Esk to its junction with a beck joining from a ravine on the left – this is **Little Narrowcove**, your route up to Scafell Pike.

The route up Little Narrowcove is less used than some other approaches to the Scafell range, and consequently lacks a consistently clear path. Use the beck as a guide, and keep above its left-hand bank. **The fairly steep ascent includes negotiating some boulders as you scramble up the ghyll, so some care will be needed.** Towards the top, as you are funnelled into the corrie, the path reappears, leading onto a seemingly insurmountable scree slope.

Fortunately, on closer inspection, the path is more defined here and weaves its way up to the pass steeply but surely.

From the pass above Little Narrowcove, head left (southwest) for 300m to the top of **Scafell Pike**. The route is easy to follow and well trodden, but take a bearing if engulfed in mist. On the summit is a trig point and a huge dry-stone memorial to soldiers lost in the Great War – and, on a clear day, views that live up to Scafell Pike's status as England's highest mountain.

To descend, from the trig point take the cairned footpath off to the northwest – the first cairn should be visible even in poor weather, and thereafter cairns are spaced regularly. After walking 300m, keep right as the cairned path splits. It's a somewhat clinical walk down, but the reassurance of a well-cairned, rocky, but easy-to-follow path may be appreciated in poor weather at the end of the day.

Continue along the stone-pitched path as it swings southwest into **Lingmell Gill**, and plod downwards. Lower down, with Wastwater filling the view ahead, you come to a dry-stone wall with a kissing gate. As you go through, look out for a path leading away from the beck, diagonally across the flank of the fell – this will take you to Wasdale Head. After a little uphill it's a gentle downhill stroll to Wasdale Head – a welcome relief after all the stone pitching. Here on the fellside you can get a shepherd's view of the mosaic of fields and walls of upper Wasdale.

WASDALE'S PATCHWORK OF FIELDS

The intricate field patterns visible at Wasdale Head today pose something of a conundrum to landscape historians. As elsewhere in the Lakes, the majority of them were built in the 18th century, but their patterns and layout hark back to an earlier age. The eminent landscape historian W. G. Hoskins attributes the tiny irregular field patterns to medieval colonisation. However, the huge girth of some of the walls perhaps suggests that the glacial fields were cleared in earlier Norse times, and that a more extensive, systematically enclosed agricultural landscape evolved in earnest from the medieval period onwards.

The fellside path comes down to meet the river at a **foot-bridge**. Cross over the bridge and into the first of Wasdale's fields and head for the road, then go right for 500m to the inn at **Wasdale Head** for a well-earned pint.

FACILITIES

Accommodation and transport
See Stage 5 on the main route.

Herdwicks by Wasdale Head Inn – Wasdale has a long history of sheep farming

HIGH LEVEL 3
Wasdale Head to Black Sail or Buttermere via Great Gable

Distance	6½ miles (10.5km) to Black Sail
	9¾ miles (15.5km) to Buttermere
Time	5–7hrs
Total ascent	1085m (3560ft)
Maps	OS 1:25,000 OL6, OL4; Harvey Superwalker West sheet
Start point	Wasdale Head, NY187087
Accommodation	Black Sail (YHA hostel only); Buttermere village
Refreshments	Buttermere village

This high-level route is an alternative to main route Stage 6 (leave at Black Sail), or to main route Stages 6 and 7 (continue to Buttermere).

Another great day of high-level walking, taking in three of Lakeland's best known peaks – Great Gable, Green Gable and Haystacks. An easy and interesting approach, walking into the morning sunlight of upper Wasdale, sets the scene. Great Gable towers over the valley to the left, with Napes Needle a reminder that this has long been a playground for climbers as well as walkers.

Half of the day's climbing is done by Sty Head pass, and a further push to the top of Gable brings you to the highpoint of the walk. Great Gable is pretty much the geographical centre of the Lake District – all the lakes radiate out from here, making the views from the summit second to none.

From Great Gable the route continues around the fells at the head of Ennerdale, making the most of height gained early in the day. It carries on to Green Gable, and finally to Haystacks, before leaving the ridgeline for either Buttermere or Black Sail.

Leave **Wasdale Head** on the footpath by the lane opposite the Barn Door shop, signed to 'St Olaf's Church'. Follow this through the fields of Herdwicks to the little church, almost hidden by the yew trees. From the back of the church, pick up the track heading leftwards – an old route over to the fells named Moses Trod. ▶

Continue on Moses Trod through the fields. On the left you may notice an exceptionally thick dry-stone wall – perhaps 5m (15ft) across – presumably a solution to the rock-strewn wastelands that must have greeted the first farmer attempting cultivation. Continue onwards through **Burnthwaite** Farm, with Moses Trod a rough cobbled track here. Cross the **footbridge** over Gable Beck, the watercourse running down from the western slopes of Great Gable to the left, and follow the left-hand bank of **Lingmell Beck** as it heads up the valley.

Reportedly Moses was a slate miner at Honister who used the route to smuggle whisky into the Wasdale valley!

Map continues p.150

To the left stand the crags of Great Gable, the names evocative of classic early climbing routes – the slim pillar of Napes Needle the most famous. Your route approaches Great Gable from its more benign eastern slopes, via Sty Head pass, which is reached by continuing up Lingmell Beck and following the trail to the top of the pass.

CLIMBING IN THE LAKE DISTRICT

Climbing as a pastime started a little later in the Lake District than in the Alps. In the late 18th century the fells were admired for their picturesque qualities, rather than as peaks to conquer. An early recorded 'climber' was Coleridge, who left the Wasdale Head Inn (then the Wastwater Hotel) in 1802 for a nine-day foray into the high fells. His resulting tales, and fame as a writer, doubtless captured the attention of numerous would-be climbers.

Many of the Lakeland peaks could be reached by walking alone, but in time interest grew in the 'impossible' peaks – those which required climbing, and where a slip meant a nasty fall. A shepherd, John Atkinson, climbed Pillar Rock, Ennerdale, in 1826, and in 1886 Hasket Smith broached Napes Needle.

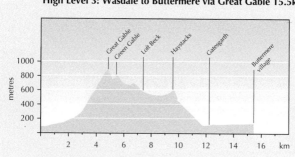

High Level 3: Wasdale to Buttermere via Great Gable 15.5km

Ennerdale from Great Gable

No mean feats in the days of hob-nailed boots! In the early 20th century the sport grew, with the formation of the Fell and Rock Climbing Club in 1907, the introduction of a grading system for routes, and the development of more modern equipment and methods. By the 1930s climbing in the Lake District was a well-established sport.

Once at **Sty Head pass**, make for the mountain rescue post, a wooden box tucked away behind a boulder. From here, two cairns 20m away to the northwest mark the start of the stone-pitched path to the summit. The pitching makes light work of the loose lower scree slopes, with cairns leading the last few metres to the summit of **Great Gable**. Its summit adornments are a little more humble than those of Scafell Pike – a discreet verdigris plate remembers those of the Fell and Rock Climbing Club who lost their lives in the First World War. ▶

This is a peaceful place to stop for lunch, reflect and enjoy the views before heading on to Green Gable.

Follow the cairned route heading northeast off the summit in the direction of nearby Green Gable. Before this next summit there is a brief drop down to Windy

149

Gap. The going for the first few metres of descent is similar to the route up, loose but substantial enough rock, and a little more easy scrambling finishes the descent to **Windy Gap**. In front now the red zigzag scar of the path up Green Gable is visible. Head up here – thankfully Green Gable is not as tall as its greater neighbour. A few minutes' walking up the red scree path leads to some cairns guiding you to the summit.

From the summit of **Green Gable** head northeast then north, following the cairns for 100m then spurring off to the left to follow the old iron boundary posts. Pass to the left of the tarns, taking the footpath skirting round the edge of **Brandreth** without actually going to the top of this particular fell. Below to the west is Ennerdale. You will meet the boundary posts again on the ridgeline – turn left on meeting these posts and follow them along.

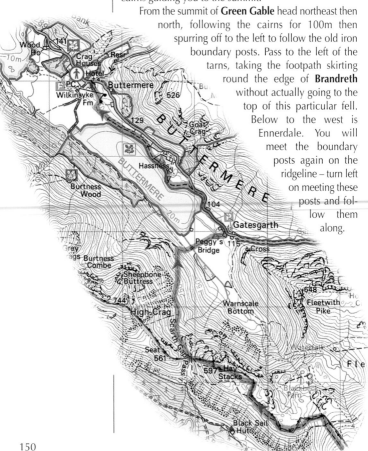

Ahead of you now, to the northwest, is Haystacks, with the innominate tarn just below its summit and the larger Black Beck tarn lower down. To the east of Haystacks is the valley of Buttermere and Crummock. Continue to follow the boundary fence, recently remade with post-and-wire fencing. You will meet the **Loft Beck** footpath coming up from Ennerdale on the left – a gravel track marked out with cairns. ▶ Where the fence-line you have been following joins a second fence heading off at right angles to the left, follow this second line to the start of the Haystacks ridgeline.

To descend to Black Sail, omitting Haystacks, take this; otherwise continue ahead along the fence-line.

Cross over the fence by a wooden stile and, using the fence-line as a wayfinder, start along the ridgeline towards Haystacks. Much of the high ground around the head of Ennerdale is owned by the National Trust and is open to public access. The route taken here is less well used, and consequently not always distinct from sheep paths on the ground, but keep just inside the fence-line until you see the **innominate tarn** over to your right. Now, head over to the tarn to pick up a more obvious rocky track from the side of the tarn up towards the summit of Haystacks.

As fans of the late Alfred Wainwright will know, this is the spot where the great walker and writer chose to have his ashes scattered. As he wrote many years before his death in 1991, 'if you dear reader should get a bit of grit in your boot as you are crossing Haystacks in the years to come, please treat it with respect. It might be me.'

And so to the summit of **Haystacks**. Perhaps summit is not the right word for it. The summit, or perhaps summits, is really an assorted collection of lumpy outcrops – the haystacks – all of broadly similar height. It really is quite an unusual fell – lower than the Gable and High Stile ranges around it, Haystacks has a homely, benign feel to it. Yet beware, some of the cairned 'routes' off the summit lead perilously close to sheer drops. Eyes first, then feet, is the order of the day as you scramble down to Scarth Gap pass.

At **Scarth Gap**, head left for Black Sail and right for Buttermere. For Black Sail, follow Loft Beck down to the

From the summit of Haystacks, with the valley of Buttermere below

head of the Ennerdale valley. A path then leads the few hundred metres to Black Sail hut. (At this point you rejoin the main route at the end of Stage 6. You can then choose whether to continue to Buttermere on the high-level route (see below), or by rejoining the main route at the start of Stage 7.) The following is the high-level route description to continue on to Buttermere.

The way down weaves through boulders – nothing technically difficult, just requiring care. In wet and misty weather the rocky pathway becomes one of an infinite number of watercourses, but thoughtfully placed cairns aid navigation. The path finally leaves the boulder field where it crosses a dry-stone wall, and soon becomes more distinct and easier underfoot as it moves into rough pasture and open fell, with the Buttermere valley unveiled beneath you.

When you reach the edge of the little plantation above the lake, take the path down to the right, which leads to **Gatesgarth Farm** via a fenced track. Turn left along the road at Gatesgarth, and follow the road until it joins the lake shore, picking up a footpath at this point.

The path heads through gorse scrub and down to the lake. By the lake shore are some beautiful craggy woodlands. Oak, beech and holly fight with the rock, and a tunnel blasted through a rocky outcrop adds a little drama to the walk as it continues to the village end of the lake.

When you come to a kissing gate towards the head of the lake, ignore a permitted path through the lakeshore fields and keep straight ahead into the woodland. A few minutes later, as you leave the trees and round a flattish rock outcrop to your right, a straight section of path leads to a junction. Take the path to the left for Buttermere village via **Wilkinsyke Farm**.

FACILITIES

Accommodation and transport
See Stages 6 and 7 in the main route.

HIGH LEVEL 4
Grasmere to Patterdale
via Helvellyn

Distance	10 miles (16km)
Time	4¾–6½hrs
Total ascent	1060m (3470ft)
Maps	OS 1:25,000 OL5, OL7; Harvey Superwalker Central sheet
Start point	Grasmere, NY337076
Accommodation	Grasmere and Patterdale
Refreshments	Patterdale

This high-level route is an alternative to the main route Stage 11.

This route provides the chance to take in Lakeland's third highest peak, Helvellyn, en route from Grasmere to Patterdale. Requiring only a little more climbing than the low-level route (which you leave behind at Grisedale Tarn) this route gets right into the thick of things, the higher sections offering interesting walking and rugged scenery in equal measure.

The approach to the Helvellyn range is determined by the route's starting point, Grasmere, and the route itself is a well-trodden, steady climb up the bank of Tongue Gill to the tarn at Grisedale Hause. A short and steep section up the flanks of Dollywagon Pike gains the day's height, and from here the legs can stretch out along the ridge to the summit of Helvellyn, with views all the way – not just of distant peaks and lakes, but of Helvellyn's many facades. Its south-western flanks are relatively gentle, leading away to Wythburn and Thirlmere below; but to the north and east Helvellyn presents its true character – the famous rocky spines of Striding Edge and Swirral Edge.

These narrow ribbons leading off the summit plateau lend the mountain drama and provide an element of excitement to the hiking – a misplaced footstep may find a sudden and near vertical shortcut to the tarn 120m below! This route takes Swirral Edge on the descent. It's moderately challenging, but for the most part not excessively exposed. Provided it is tackled in good weather, and not in high winds or winter conditions, it should be rewarding rather than frightening. Swirral Edge is also realistic with full packs, although dog owners may have to carry their loved ones over one or two of the larger boulders.

From the centre of **Grasmere**, take the Easedale road opposite the bookshop in the centre of the village, passing the entrance to Butterlyp How Youth Hostel. Shortly afterwards, a permitted path to the left of the road avoids the tarmac for a few hundred metres before rejoining the Easedale road. Look out for a small lane off to the right (you will see a sign indicating a second youth hostel) and follow this lane all the way down to **Low Mill bridge**, then head right to meet the main Ambleside–Keswick road.

Map continues p.156

Cross the main road to follow the bridleway opposite, signed to Patterdale. The way starts as a quiet lane passing through some houses, ascending steadily on a cobbled track amidst bracken, with Tongue Gill bubbling away 100m or so below. The beck is named after the elongated fell ahead, which you reach after 800m of walking from the main road. Here at the base of Great Tongue you will see a footbridge to the left and one to the right; take the right-hand one. Now follow **Tongue Gill** as the ravine heads up the right-hand side of the Tongue. Immediately after the footbridge you will come to an iron-railed compound housing a

155

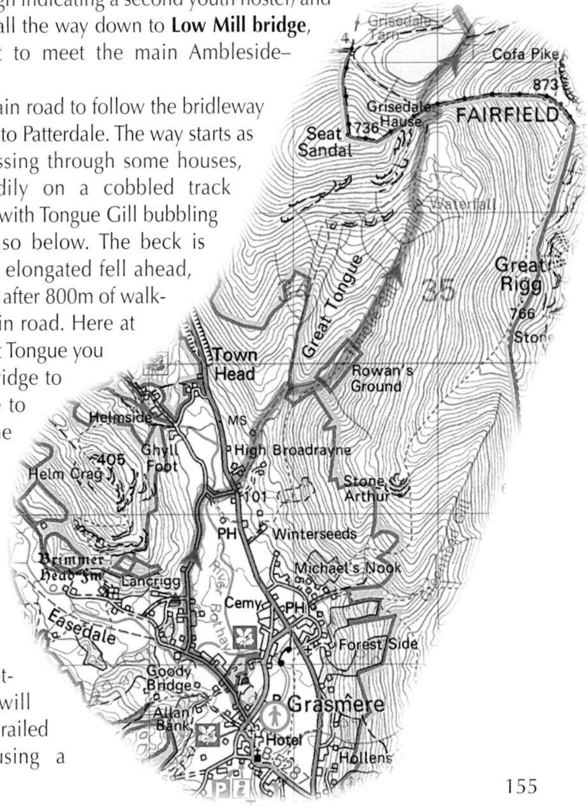

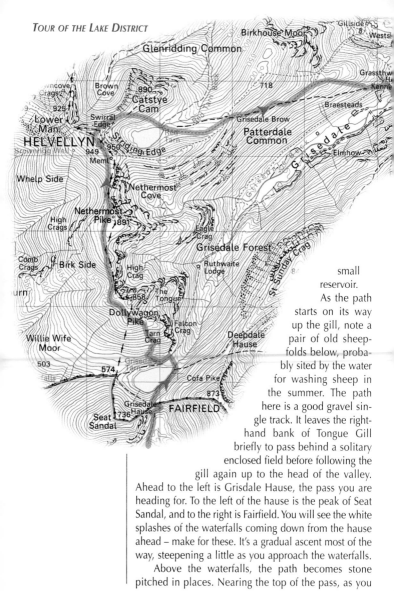

small
reservoir.

As the path starts on its way up the gill, note a pair of old sheep-folds below, probably sited by the water for washing sheep in the summer. The path here is a good gravel single track. It leaves the right-hand bank of Tongue Gill briefly to pass behind a solitary enclosed field before following the gill again up to the head of the valley. Ahead to the left is Grisdale Hause, the pass you are heading for. To the left of the hause is the peak of Seat Sandal, and to the right is Fairfield. You will see the white splashes of the waterfalls coming down from the hause ahead – make for these. It's a gradual ascent most of the way, steepening a little as you approach the waterfalls.

Above the waterfalls, the path becomes stone pitched in places. Nearing the top of the pass, as you

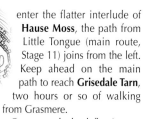

enter the flatter interlude of **Hause Moss**, the path from Little Tongue (main route, Stage 11) joins from the left. Keep ahead on the main path to reach **Grisedale Tarn**, two hours or so of walking from Grasmere.

Cross over the beck flowing out of Grisedale Tarn and take the path heading up Dollywagon Pike, heading leftward initially up the flank of the fellside. The route zigzags up the slopes, climbing steadily, and after a boggy start by the tarn soon turns into a good path, a mixture of gravel and stone pitching. The summit of **Dollywagon** is bypassed, the path keeping a little below and to the left, then meeting the remains of the boundary fence – now a solitary iron post in the middle of the track. Contour round the back of the summit, towards High Crag and Nethermost Pike.

The path dips a little from Dollywagon before climbing up behind **High Crag**, and the sides of the path are littered with friable slate. It is quite a wide track here, very easy to follow and cairned in places beyond High Crag. Carry onwards across the broad plateau of

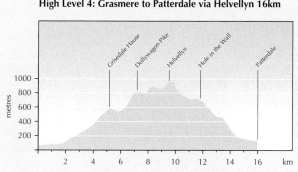

High Level 4: Grasmere to Patterdale via Helvellyn 16km

Nethermost Pike, dipping briefly again before climbing up to the summit of Helvellyn itself. As you climb into this last dip, ahead is a neatly framed view of the triangular profile of Catstye Cam in the background, then the ragged line of Striding Edge is revealed in the foreground to the immediate right. Your route along Swirral Edge towards Catstye Cam is still hidden at this point. And so continue to the summit of **Helvellyn**.

Near the summit is a commemorative plaque to the first aircraft to land on a British mountain, flown by two brave lads back in 1926 who must have timed their attempt very well to land on a wind-free day! A star-shaped stone shelter by the summit provides some respite for today's visitors, who may not be so lucky with the weather. Continue on to the trig point. Some 200m

Grisedale valley, without a tarred road – much of the valley is accessible only on foot

Swirral Edge in winter – strictly for the climbers!

from this, on the edge of the summit plateau, stands a cairn on the loose stone. This marks the start of the descent along Swirral Edge.

The first few metres of the scramble down onto **Swirral Edge** are moderately challenging, but the going soon gets easier, as the route reverts to walking rather than scrambling. A narrow gravel path leads the way along the ridge, with Catstye Cam straight ahead and Red Tarn far below to the right at the base of the crags. When you reach the high point in the middle of Swirral Edge, look out for a the path leading off the ridge to the right, heading down to the end of Red Tarn. Take this, leaving Catstye Cam for another day.

HELVELLYN – A CAUTIONARY TALE

A third summit memorial on Helvellyn retells perhaps the most famous story associated with the mountain, that of the unfortunate Charles Gough and his terrier Foxey, who set out one day in spring 1805 from Patterdale to Wythburn. As can often happen at this time of year, snow obscured the path, and thus a disoriented Gough plunged to his death on the crags above Red Tarn. His body was not found until three months later, when all that remained was his bleached white bones beneath his clothing. Remarkably his dog Foxey was still keeping vigil over her master, inspiring verses on the subject of loyalty from Wordsworth and Scott. From other quarters, there were less kindly suggestions that she must have eaten Gough herself!

As you get close to **Red Tarn**, a path joins yours from the left. Turn right here, heading towards the tarn. Cross the beck flowing out of the tarn, and now pick up the path heading diagonally across the fell in front of you to **Hole in the Wall** – you will see the wall if not the hole. This is where we meet the path leading down from Striding Edge.

At Hole in the Wall cross over the ladder-stile to the other side of the wall, and follow the path heading left and downhill. It's a stone-pitched path, winding down the slope into the **Grisedale valley**. The path is obvious and easy to follow, a chance to enjoy some great views without concentrating so much on where to put your feet! Continue through several kissing gates. Lower down, when your path reaches a gate in a wall by some Scots pine trees, go through and head down to the tarred lane below. Follow the lane across the river, and at the junction 50m beyond the bridge turn left on the tarred lane heading down the valley. At a left-hand bend in the road, 800m downhill, take a signed footpath to the right past some farm buildings. Go through a gate into a field on the left, and walk over a grassy hillock and over a wall stile at the far end of the field. Once over the stile, turn left and head downhill through the birch trees to the village of **Patterdale**.

<hr>

FACILITIES

Accommodation and transport
See Stage 11 in the main route.

HIGH LEVEL 5
Patterdale to Windermere
via High Street

Distance	14 miles (23km)
Time	6–8hrs
Total ascent	1015m (3340ft)
Maps	OS 1:25,000 OL5, OL7; Harvey Superwalker East and South East sheets
Start point	Patterdale, NY397159
Accommodation	Windermere
Refreshments	Patterdale, Troutbeck (+1 mile), Windermere town

This high-level route is an alternative to the main route Stage 12.

This long day in the fells is a fitting finale to a walking trip through the Lake District. High Street, the fell named after the Roman road crossing its summit, is the highest fell east of the Kirkstone Pass and consequently enjoys uninterrupted views for many miles from its vast summit plateau. As well as an important route to the Romans, part of the fell known as Racecourse Hill has been a somewhat unlikely pleasure spot in more recent history. In the 19th century it was popular for a while to hold horse racing and Cumberland wrestling competitions in this natural arena, 3000ft up from the valley floor!

There is of course some climbing today, but of the steady variety, with the effort spread over the several miles from Patterdale. Once on the High Street summit ridge, there is a long, almost level section to enjoy as far as Thornthwaite Beacon, requiring little effort. A short but somewhat steep descent into Troutbeck will try tired leg muscles, but from here its lowland walking, back to the starting point of the Tour at Windermere.

From the post office in **Patterdale**, continue in the direction of Glenridding on the road, passing the Patterdale Hotel on your left and the small car park and bus stop on the right. Take the next right, a bridleway signed to **Side Farm**, also a campsite. On reaching the farm buildings, turn right through the farm gate to follow the bridleway, shortly passing another cottage on the left. Go on through a second field gate onto a tarred lane – turn immediately left here, following the sign to Angle Tarn. The gravel track winds up from the trees to the bracken-covered fellside above. As the track gains height on its way to Boredale Hause, views of Ullswater and Patterdale open up behind, and Brotherswater is glimpsed ahead. Where the track splits, take either option – the two join and continue to Boredale Hause.

On reaching **Boredale Hause** you are greeted with a confusion of paths. Ignore the first footpath on the right

Ullswater from Side Farm, a campsite right by the lake shore near Patterdale

leading downhill toward Brotherswater. Instead take the second one on the right, crossing the beck ahead by a sheepfold and heading up into the hills. The path climbs up through rough grazing land on a distinct path. After a little uphill walking some cairns lead through a ravine, at the top of which the Angletarn Pikes come into view in the distance over to the left. You now head towards these. Approaching the Pikes, you come to a fork in the path. Take the left-hand option, which comes close to these craggy peaks, before contouring right-wards around their base. Now **Angle Tarn** comes into view below.

Head along the path to the left of the tarn, now on a flattish section of trail. Over to your right, beyond the tarn, you will see Cat and Broad Crags. From the tarn, the path (now stone pitched in places) gains more height and is easy to follow. Some 600m from the tarn, at a crossing of dry-stone walls, take the path to the left-hand side of the wall ahead, and follow it over the lump of **Satura Crag**. Where this dry-stone wall turns into

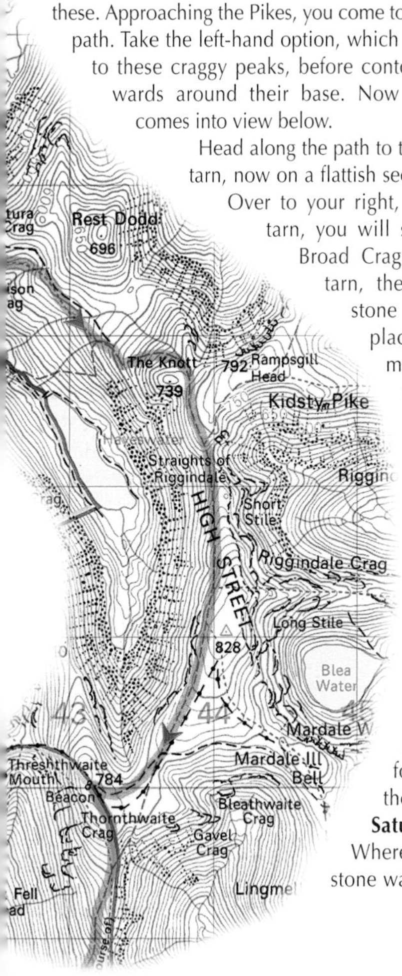

Map continues p.165

163

a fence, make sure you continue to follow the fence-line rather than taking the path heading over the hummock to the left leading to the summit of Rest Dodd. Below, you will see Hayeswater, and the path loses height as it heads into its valley a little before contouring round the base of **Rest Dodd**.

In the ravine between Rest Dodd and the Knott you will come to a dry-stone wall – the going here is a bit boggy, but is partially flagged with stone slabs. Head through the wall and start climbing up the side of the **Knott** on the easy-to-follow path (cairned in places). As you get higher up the slope you will see another wall in front of you, which you cross later on. A bridleway from Hayeswater joins your path from the right; turn left here and keep heading upwards. When the path crosses the wall, follow the cairned route – you pass to the north of the Knott's summit. On reaching a wall coming down to your path from the summit on your right, keep straight on. Your path now leads on to the **Straights of Riggindale**.

On the Straights of Riggindale, 600m from the Knott, you may see a path leading off to Kidsty Pike on the left. Ignore this (the Coast to Coast route) and carry on ahead, on a downhill section. Shortly afterwards, on a low point on the ridge, pass through the wall as the path starts to

High Level 5: Patterdale to Windermere via High Street 23km

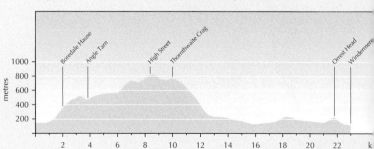

164

climb gently again onto High Street, heading a little away from the wall now. The track is quite wide along here.

The official summit of **High Street** is 200m off to the left of the track, but return to the main track as it starts to descend. After approximately 800m of gentle downhill walking along the wide track, you come to a wall crossing the way at NY436102. Here, continue on the broad stony track which continues to descend for a few more minutes before rising to the prominent beacon **on Thornthwaite Crag**. The impressive tower of stone, higher than a man and solidly built, overlooks the head of Troutbeck valley – your next destination before Windermere.

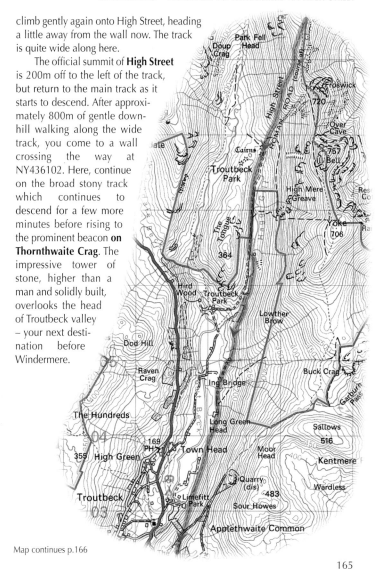

Map continues p.166

165

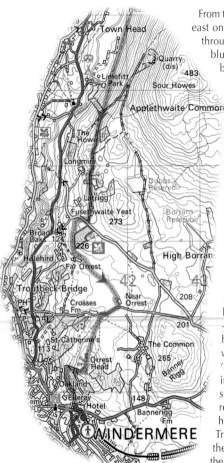

From the beacon, the path goes south-east on a well-used route descending through the grassy fellside. The long blue streak of Windermere is visible in the distance to the right, and ahead lies the rugged ridgeline of Froswick, Ill Bell and Yoke. After 200m gentle walking from the beacon, the path starts to descend more rapidly to the col between these three peaks and the High Street range. At the lowest point in the col, look out for the path heading right, and take this to enter the Troutbeck valley by the slopes of **Park Fell**.

The descent of Park Fell's grass-covered slopes reveals the head of the Troutbeck valley, and some familiar landmarks beyond. The names on the map – Park Fell and Troutbeck Park – hark back to an era when this was a royal hunting ground. 'Forest' (or 'park') here has nothing to do with trees; it means simply an area managed and reserved for the privileged hunters. To the right, beyond the Troutbeck valley, are Red Screes, the Kirkstone Pass and the scar of the slate quarry. Further afield, and visible on a clear day, are Coniston Old Man and the Furness fells, leading away to the coast at Morecambe Bay.

After a gentle start, the descent of Park Fell becomes quite steep, although its grassy slopes make for a relatively painless descent – compared to the tortuous stone pitching on earlier peaks! Where the path meets **Hagg Gill** at a gate in a dry-stone wall, the gradient relents. From here the path follows a farmer's track, with Hagg Beck just a few metres over to your left. After passing the first two enclosed fields immediately to the left of the track, look out for a stone barn. Turn off the main track here, taking a track to the left, and cross the beck by a footbridge by the barn. Continue down the valley on this far side of Hagg Beck.

Go through a gate on the track by a hawthorn bush above a second footbridge. Now in the bottom of the valley, continue along the track for a mile **to Long Green Head Farm**. The bridleway continues past the farm. At a fork in the track above Limefitt **caravan park**, keep left and slightly uphill. After a field gate the track merges with the Garburn Pass trail coming in from the left. Very shortly afterwards the path ahead forks – take the left-hand option, slightly uphill. Keep on the track until you reach the Troutbeck–Ings Road at a **T-junction**. Great views of Windermere are now revealed ahead.

At this T-junction, turn right to head downhill for 200m, before picking up the footpath to Far Orrest on

Troutbeck and The Tongue from Kirkstone Road – a different view of the valley from this vantage point

the left side of the road. Follow the footpath, in time coming to a field gate leading into a lonnin to Far Orrest. Instead of crossing the farm at **Far Orrest**, take the footpath just before it to the left which heads to Near Orrest, clipping the edge of the field before going through two sets of kissing gates guarding another lonnin.

From the kissing gates go through a field and over a ladder-stile, and through three similar fields with ladder or stone stiles. Then over a stone stile, and ditto. Then go through a kissing gate before **Near Orrest Farm**. Here head to another kissing gate to the right of the farm, where the path emerges onto a tarred lane. Turn right to follow the lane for 200m before picking up a footpath to the left to Orrest Head and Windermere. Follow a path leading to the top for a last well-earned pause at the **Orrest Head** viewpoint, before saying your farewells to the fells and heading downhill at the far side. The path will lead you back to your starting point, **Windermere** railway station.

FACILITIES

Accommodation and transport
See Stage 12 in the main route.

PART 4
SHORT WALKS

The waterfalls at Stock Ghyll are only a few minutes' walk from Ambleside (Short Walk 2)

SHORT WALK 1

*Beatrix Potter's Hill Top and Claife
Heights from the Windermere ferry*

Start/finish	Ferry House, Sawrey, SD390957
Time	3hrs
Distance	7 miles (11km)
Total ascent	315m (1030ft)
Parking	Harrow Slack, SD387960, NT, Pay and Display
	Claife Station, SD387953, NT, Pay and Display
	Red Nab, SD385994, NT, free (+1.5km)
Buses/ferry	The 599 bus service from Windermere station to
	Bowness, frequent
	Ferry service every 20mins between Bowness and
	Ferry House, Sawrey
Refreshments	Near and Far Sawrey
Maps	OS 1:25,000 OL7, Harvey Superwalker
	South East sheet

This walk is accessible from Windermere, on Stages 1 and 12 of the main route.

This very varied walk reaches Hill Top, one of Lakeland's main visitor attractions, by usually quiet trails. Beginning at Ferry House, Sawrey, there is a chance to get acquainted with England's largest lake on its less touristed western shore. At Belle Grange the route turns away from Windermere and heads up into woodlands – the lower slopes of the Claife estate are covered with old coppice woodlands, carpeted with bluebells in the spring. Climbing further, it enters conifer plantations – red squirrel and pine marten territory – before emerging from the trees for panoramic views of the Furness hills. There is a chance for refreshments at Near Sawrey before a visit to Beatrix Potter's Hill Top, then a pleasant potter back through the fields to catch the ferry back to Bowness.

Leaving the ferry at **Ferry House**, walk along the access road a few metres to pick up a footpath to the right, leading through the grounds of the former Freshwater

Biological Station at the end of the lake. The footpath
brings you out on a small lane skirting the lake shore,
used for launching boats. Turn right along here, past a
National Trust car park at **Harrow Slack**, and the road
becomes an unsurfaced track after a time. Pass to the left
of the Trust's Strawberry Gardens caravan park and head
into the lakeside woodlands. At a wildlife viewing platform (where you may catch a glimpse of red squirrels)
keep on the main track downhill, which leads on to **Belle
Grange**.

At Belle Grange pick up a finger-posted bridleway
signed 'Hawkshead 3 miles' to the left, leading away
from the lake shore on a stone-flagged path through the
woodlands of the National Trust's Claife estate. After 10
minutes or so of walking the gradient levels out slightly.
Ignore the public footpath off to the left, and instead
carry on uphill following the sign 'Hawkshead via Guide
Posts'. The track is now gravel underfoot, blanketed with
pine needles, and a little boggy in places.

COPPICING IN THE SOUTH LAKES

This old area of hazel coppice, with sessile oak over-
head, is typical of traditional South Lakeland managed
woodlands. Fast-growing species such as hazel and
willow were cut close to the ground on a rotational
basis, every 5 to 10 years. The cut stumps then sprout
harvestable straight poles useful for various purposes,
from firewood to rural crafts, including willow bas-
ketry and making hazel besoms.

This method of growing small timber quickly was
a key part of the local economy in the days of the thriv-
ing Lancashire cotton industry – the woods supplying
the bobbins for the mills. A second, complementary
industry of the coppice woodlands was charcoal burn-
ing, again a craft dying with its market, although there
is now a small-scale resurgence in producing environ-
mentally sound barbecue fuel!

Today these woodlands are valuable as an eco-
logical resource – the mixture of hazel coppice, oak

On the track from Sawrey onto Claife Heights, a gate leads to the tarns, with the Langdale Pikes in background

standards and scattered birch, holly and rowan here, for example, creating a diverse, multi-layered habitat.

The path now enters a part of the forest dominated by coniferous species before the trees break at a large collection of signs on a forest track. Choose the option to 'Sawrey via the Tarns' ahead to the left.

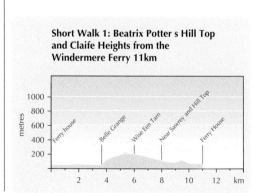

Short Walk 1: Beatrix Potter s Hill Top and Claife Heights from the Windermere Ferry 11km

BEATRIX POTTER AND HAWKSHEAD

You could at this point opt to head down to the village of Hawkshead. With St Michael's Church overlooking the cobbled medieval streets around the square and connections with Wordsworth and Beatrix Potter, it is well worth a visit. Beatrix Potter's gallery in the village (National Trust, Easter to October, Monday to Thursday and Sunday 10.30am-4.30pm) holds some interesting examples of the watercolours illustrating the tales – images you can then relate to real scenes around the village. If you choose to walk down to Hawkshead, you might pick up the bus to rejoin the walk at Hill Top in Near Sawrey. But time this carefully – the bus service runs only three times a day even in the summer!

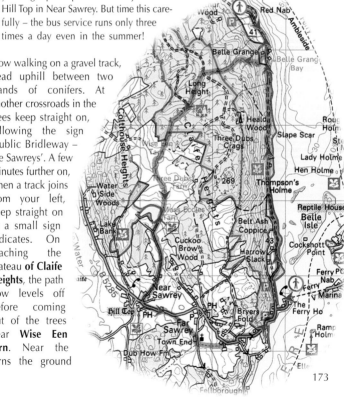

Now walking on a gravel track, head uphill between two stands of conifers. At another crossroads in the trees keep straight on, following the sign 'Public Bridleway – the Sawreys'. A few minutes further on, when a track joins from your left, keep straight on as a small sign indicates. On reaching the plateau **of Claife Heights**, the path now levels off before coming out of the trees near **Wise Een tarn**. Near the tarns the ground

173

Before going through the field gate, turn round for a last look at the tarns, with a beautifully framed view of the Langdale Pikes on the horizon.

Refreshments: Tower Bank Arms, Near Sawrey. Pub food and snacks.

can be very boggy. Your path goes to the right of the smaller tarn at Wise Een, then heads leftwards and upwards – an easy-to-follow track. ◄

Keep on going down, passing **Moss Eccles tarn** to your right, where the track is channelled between two dry-stone walls at a field gate. Where the track splits, take the right-hand fork to Near Sawrey. On reaching the road by the post box in the village, turn left past the Tower Bank Arms, 50m beyond which is **Hill Top**. ◄

BEATRIX POTTER'S HILL TOP

Mrs Heelis, known to the wider world as Beatrix Potter, bought the farm at Hill Top with the proceeds of her first books, and it is here that she developed her passion for farming and the breeding of Herdwick sheep in particular. As a condition of her bequest to the National Trust, the house and its contents are kept today much as they were during her time in Sawrey, and are open to the public every day except Thursday and Friday, Easter to October, 10.30am–4.30pm.

Follow the road for a further 50m beyond Hill Top to pick up a permissive path to the right, avoiding the traffic. When, after a few hundred metres, the path passes through a gate to a footbridge leading back to the road, keep on the footpath signed in both English and Japanese to the ferry. This permissive path route misses Far Sawrey, and heads off instead in the direction of the church.

On reaching the tarred lane under the **church** turn right and take a footpath signed to Bryers Fold just beyond the churchyard's boundary wall. Continue through a kissing gate and into a second field, following the boundary up on the right-hand side. Where the post-and-wire fence meets a short section of wall, go through another gate and follow the path through a third kissing gate, shortly to meet the road down to the ferry.

You now have to walk down the road for a while, which can be busy at times. Just after the Far Sawrey village sign there is, however, a permitted footpath you can take on the right-hand side of the road. At the entrance of the National Trust's **Ash Landing** nature reserve, cross over the road to pick up the continued permitted path at the other side. Another 100m of walking brings you to a small National Trust car park. Walk through this to a public footpath continuing down to the ferry. A second public footpath shortly afterwards on the left takes you up to the ruin of **Claife Station** visible above, and then down to the lakeside road at the ferry road junction. Claife Station was built in the 1790s – not for trains but as a viewing station from which to see the lake in its most picturesque aspect. Continue along the lakeside road, and 100m from here the footpath to the right leads back through the grounds of the research station to **Ferry House**.

A robin singing for a mate on a signpost at Belle Grange

SHORT WALK 2
Stock Ghyll, Scandale and High Sweden Bridge from Ambleside

Start/finish	Market Hall, Ambleside, NY377044
Time	2½hrs
Distance	5 miles (8.5km)
Total ascent	340m (1120ft)
Parking	Ambleside, NY374047, Pay and Display
Buses/ferry	Ambleside is on the frequent 555 Lakeslink bus route
Refreshments	Ambleside – numerous cafes and pubs
Maps	OS 1:25,000 OL7, Harvey Superwalker Central sheet

This easy half-day walk, or evening stroll in the summer, takes you out of town and away from the crowds. Although it has its picture-postcard moments – High Sweden Bridge, and the 20m (60ft) cascade at Stock Ghyll – it is primarily a walk through workaday farming Ambleside, on less visited paths. As Ambleside goes, this is as about as far from the tourist crowds as it gets.

There is some tarmac to deal with at the start, but the going for much of the route is easy and firm, at low level, making it a good wet-weather option – any extra water only adds to the drama of the waterfalls!

The waters of Stock Ghyll were once the power supply of Ambleside, and Stock Ghyll was the site of the town's first corn mill, built in 1324. The name 'Stock Ghyll' itself is an interesting example of language evolving – 'gill' is from the Norse for 'ravine', but 'ghyll' is an alternate spelling invented or at least popularised by Wordsworth. The 'stock' element is from the Old English, meaning simply 'wood' – hence 'wooded ravine'.

Behind the former market hall next to Barclays Bank pick up the lane heading uphill where a sign in the wall directs 'to the waterfalls'. The lane follows Stock Ghyll, lined with broadleaf woodlands. Keep walking up the lane for 400m to reach the entrance to **Stock Ghyll Park** on the left, leading to the waterfalls. Follow the red arrows to the falls. This being the Lake District, there is

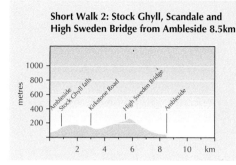

**Short Walk 2: Stock Ghyll, Scandale and
High Sweden Bridge from Ambleside 8.5km**

usually an impressive amount of water crashing down the ghyll. Having arrived at the base of the largest of the falls, follow the signs to the revolving exit on the lane-side. ▶

Follow the public footpath sign uphill past a wooden seat. Although the lane from here up to Grove Farm is now tarred, it is actually only a right of way for pedestrians, so you should enjoy a traffic-free stroll. The ghyll is now roaring away down below you now. (**Note:** do not take the footpath to Troutbeck via Wansfell off to the right, but continue along the lane.) Walk over a cattle grid and past a derelict farm building on your left. A tree-lined gill cuts over and under the lane, and soon you approach the buildings of **Low Grove House**.

As you go through the gate by the cattle grid at Low Grove House you will see a footpath leading off through the field on the left. Take this, and go through

There are several good viewpoints as you climb through holly, oak and beech woodland, with daffodils in the spring.

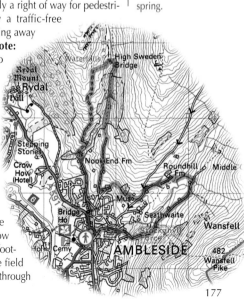

Stock Ghyll waterfall is nestled amidst a primrose woodland

a gate by a paling fence at the bottom of the field to cross a small sleeper bridge. Take an obvious path at the far side of the bridge, following the bank of Stock Ghyll for a few metres. Ignore the kissing gate, and instead hairpin uphill to the right up to the farmyard of **Roundhill Farm**.

Follow the farm lane out, and after 350m join the **Kirkstone Pass road**. Head down the road for 250m, and where it veers round to the right pick up the wooden fin-ger-posted path to Ellerigg. This is a marvellous old-style lane lined with rambling, wavy moss-covered walls, with Ambleside visible below.

When you reach a field gate with a 'no dogs' sign on it, leave the main track to take a smaller footpath close to the wall on the left, and go through a squeeze-stile at the far end. Another small gated stile leads onto a path by the house of Ellerigg. As you weave through the first houses and round a bend to see the Ellerigg sub-station, take the lane off to the right. This connects to another walled, lane leading uphill. Follow this for 75m to a gate on the lane, whereafter it becomes cobbled. Keep on heading up, with a wall on both sides.

Pass a long-abandoned farm building on the right. Its entrances are now closed in, and the whole building has melded into the wall – it would have been quite an isolated spot to farm in the past! Just before entering some birch and ash woodland, the sound of water reaches your ears – this is Scandale Beck, the second ghyll of the day. It's a ruggedly picturesque spot, with cascading waters and trees clinging to the ravine – all the more so when shrouded in mist. To the right of the path you pass two tortured grottoes, former small quarry workings.

As you leave the woodland and splash over a tributary beck joining from the right, you come to **High Sweden Bridge**, stone built in the packhorse style.

STONE GATE POSTS

As you pass through the small gate at the far side of the bridge, pause for a second to look at the two old stone gate posts with their round holes. The pair are a good example of an old style of simple gate. The holes would have taken wooden poles cut from coppiced trees – the thin end pushed into the round hole, and the thick end squared off to jam in the hole at the other side. Hence the expression 'a square peg in a round hole'. The lowest pole could be removed to let the small lambs through to fresh grass, while holding the older sheep back.

Once over the bridge, turn left to follow the single-track path as it winds up along a decaying wall to the first ridge on the hillside to reach a ladder-stile. Beyond the stile continue straight ahead, gaining height to a T-junction of footpaths by a **sheepfold**. Turn left and start to head downhill. After 20m the fairly wide track heads through a defined gap in the wall and enters a marshy area. Keep on heading downhill on the meandering double track, and eventually the walls move aside to show Ambleside below.

LOW AND HIGH SWEDEN BRIDGES

The 'Sweden' in the name Sweden Bridge is something of a red herring, having nothing to do with Sweden at all. The origins of the name are tied up with the early transhumance sheep farming practised by the descendants of the Norse settlers. To move stock up to the summer pastures above the bracken and scrub, pathways were cleared. In late spring these pathways might be burned to encourage fresh grass that the flock could later graze on as they moved back down in the winter. This type of burnt pathway is 'swarthens' in old Norse. Hence, the route up to the summer shielings above Ambleside was known, until the early 19th century, as Swarthen Way. John Carnie, in his book *At Lakeland's Heart*, suggests that the name was changed in the 1840s to 'Sweden' on the whim of Ambleside's first property developer – perhaps it sounded more exotic!

The track becomes more secure and solid as you descend – the latter section almost suburban as it hairpins down to **Low Sweden Bridge**. This second bridge has some pretty impressive cascades running underneath, and it's a real thrill to grip to the handrail when the beck is in spate! Head through two gates onto a tarred lane by the farm, and head downhill to **Ambleside**, reaching the town by the St Martin's College buildings. Before heading off you might consider visiting Ambleside's Lakes Discovery Museum, just to the right by the main road. The museum is open daily 10am–5pm, and focuses on the artists and intellectuals of the area. Exhibits include correspondence from Ruskin, Beatrix Potter watercolours and a Roman collection from R. G. Collingwood.

SHORT WALK 3
*Elterwater – a riverside walk
between two pubs*

Start/finish	Britannia Pub, Elterwater, NY327048
Time	3½hrs
Distance	7½ miles (12km)
Total ascent	305m (990ft)
Parking	Elterwater, NY327047, NT, Pay and Display
	Elterwater Common, NY329051, free
Buses	Elterwater is on the infrequent 516
	Langdale bus service
Refreshments	Britannia Inn, Elterwater
	Old Dungeon Ghyll, Langdale
	New Dungeon Ghyll, Langdale
	Brambles Cafe, Chapel Stile
Maps	OS 1:25,000 OL6, Harvey Superwalker Central sheet

This good half-day walk is best timed to coincide with opening hours at either of the two particularly noteworthy pubs en route – The Britannia by the green in Elterwater and the Old Dungeon Ghyll at the end of the Langdale valley. The Britannia does a good line in traditional Lakeland food washed down with real ales, while the ODG (as it is sometimes abbreviated) just has to be visited for its stripped down, climbing ambience – or simply a restorative pint by the open fire.

This walk also gives a good insight into the history of the Langdale valley, leading as it does through past and present quarries, into coppiced woodlands, and by riverside meadows and farms. There's even a brief stop-off in pre-history at Copt Howe, site of some remarkable marked boulders. Rocks and boulders are something of a theme for the day, for the glaciers certainly left their mark on this particular valley.

From the National Trust car park opposite the Britannia Inn, cross over Elterwater Bridge and turn onto the tarred lane off to the right by the riverside. There is evidence of slate quarrying all around here – Elterwater's money earner before the arrival of the tourists. Over the hill to the left is the main quarry which you will see later, and across the river is the Langdale timeshare village, roofed in Elterwater slate. Opposite a quarried cave 150m down the lane, pick up a footpath leading down to the riverside. You might see kingfishers and dippers down here.

You shortly reach the footbridge on the outskirts of **Chapel Stile**. Do not cross over, but instead head round to the left to keep to a footpath by the wall. With big slate spoil heaps to the left, the path leaves the riverside to head into the slate mine between two enormous dry-stone gable ends. Head on up to the first quarry buildings following an iron water pipe. There is an information board

Elterwater quarry, a scene of eerie grandeur

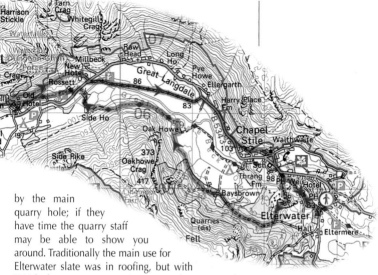

by the main
quarry hole; if they
have time the quarry staff
may be able to show you
around. Traditionally the main use for
Elterwater slate was in roofing, but with
British slate now an expensive commodity, new markets
are being found in luxury flooring. Follow the public footpath signs past the Burlington Slate office and into the
woodland beyond on a good gravel track.

When the track climbs a little to reach a T-junction
with a larger lane by a house, turn right. This is marked
as unsurfaced road on the OS maps, but has since been

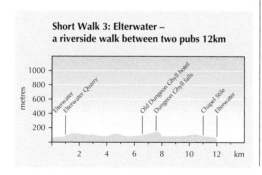

**Short Walk 3: Elterwater –
a riverside walk between two pubs 12km**

tarred. Continue through the old oak and hazel coppice woodland to **Baysbrown** to pick up a bridleway on the left-hand side of the farmyard. Continue on this double-track bridleway, keeping left when it is split 100m from the farm by two boulders. These are two of many glacial erratics left in the valley since the last Ice Age. Shortly after this there is a bridleway signed off to the right – take this, through some larch trees.

The houses of Chapel Stile and Great Langdale are visible to the right, and over to the left are continuing signs of past mining efforts. Leaving the trees after a while, you enter an area where it seems the giants have been throwing rocks around – or more that farmers over the centuries have preferred to work around the glacial boulders rather than move them. Here you pass through a field gate into rough grazing land, with patches of grass between the bracken. Keep on this path as it starts to descend to **Oak Howe** farm house, with its white gable end.

Reaching the barn at Oak Howe, turn left onto the public footpath heading off in the direction of the

Langdale and the Pikes

Langdale Pikes – Pavey Ark and Harrison Stickle neatly framed before you. Continue on this easy-to-follow path as it comes down to meet Great Langdale Beck. The path follows the wall line, hopping over streams, until eventually some stone pitching takes you down from the intake wall **to Side House**, entering the farmyard by a kissing gate. Head right here, and go onto the lane leading to the Langdale road. Cross over and into the National Trust car park. As you go into Stickle Ghyll car park, find a little footpath tucked away in the left-hand corner. This takes you over a stile and climbs up through a few small trees above the car park. Immediately above these trees turn left through a hole in the wall on an obvious path into a field.

From here the path is less defined and, unusually for the Lake District, poorly signed. Cross the sleeper bridge and ignore a tractor-crossing bridge down to the left. Instead, keeping to the bottom half of the field, cross a tributary stream by a slate sleeper to find a wooden stile in the bottom left corner of the field, right by the bank of Langdale Beck. From this stile it is straight across to a field gate in the middle of the wall at the far side, and signs appear again. The path now is more defined, and brings you to a meadow in front of the **Old Dungeon Ghyll hotel**. ▶

Leave the Old Dungeon Ghyll by the back of the hotel, taking the gated entrance to the Mickleden footpath, but doing an immediate hairpin turn uphill to get on the lonnin heading back down the valley. This footpath is easier to follow and more used than the one you took earlier, and has gravel underfoot. You will pass the Dungeon Ghyll itself, crossing the waters by a little wooden footbridge. ▶

From the bridge, the path keeps close to the wall on the right to reach the brow before dropping sharply down to Stickle Ghyll and the **New Dungeon Ghyll hotel**. Head straight out along the driveway to the New Dungeon Ghyll and cross into the triangular LDNP car park. Pick up the track from the left-hand corner of the parking area, which you follow for 1.5km until it rejoins

Refreshments:
Old Dungeon Ghyll hotel – hikers' bar serving bar snacks and coffees.

There is a second vantage point a few metres upstream.

the main road by a lovely George V post box embedded in the wall.

Turn right on the main road, noting a bridleway off to the right after 200m leading to Elterwater – you could take this for a riverside stroll back to the start. The main route described here continues a little further along the road to Copt Howe, but if the traffic is busy you might consider returning to Elterwater by the riverside instead.

As you continue down the road, just past the bridleway you will see slates embedded vertically in the fields as a boundary fence. Over on the other side of the road, walls have been built around and on glacial boulders – boulders which have probably shifted no more than a few feet (if at all) in millennia! **Pass Harry Place Farm** on the left, a handsome whitewashed house. On the right, a couple of fields beyond the last of the farm buildings, a small gate on the right leads into the Copt Howe boulders.

COPT HOWE –
A TALE OF TWO BOULDERS

Long used as a playground by local climbers to practise their skills, it wasn't until as recently as 1999 that two archaeologists, Paul and Barbara Brown, recognised the Copt Howe boulders for what they are – one of Lakeland's most important prehistoric sites. It is perhaps unsurprising that the carvings of concentric rings and linear motifs had gone unnoticed – they are in most lights indistinct, but go to the boulders in low, morning light to see them revealed.

Previously, markings of this type had only been found on the periphery of the Lake District, but the close proximity of the Neolithic 'axe factory' at Pike o'Stickle may offer a clue to the origin of these markings. Copt Howe may have been a finishing site, where the rough-outs were honed to a finished axe. Or, as some have more fancifully suggested, the markings may represent a Neolithic map of the Langdale valley, depicting the location of the axe factory and routes through the area.

Just off the busy Langdale road are the Copt Howe boulders

Until recent times, the lower Langdale valley was an extensive floodplain – now the fields by Great Langdale Beck have been drained. In Neolithic times, Copt Howe would have stood on the edge of a marsh. From here axes could have been transported from the fells to the coast via Elterwater and Windermere by canoe.

By the way, in an effort to conserve the markings, climbing is now actively discouraged!

Continue along towards the houses of Chapel Stile, by the road. Approximately 100m past the village limit signs, leave the road by a footpath off to the left, which becomes a grassy lane above a row of slate cottages. The path leads to a slate outcrop and former quarries, with views over the Chapel Stile area. Continue along the footpath as it picks its way down through the quarry, popping out at **Chapel Stile** in a quiet corner by the church. From here, work your way downhill, reaching the Langdale road by Brambles cafe and post office. ▶

Turn left along the main road, and continue along to join a bridleway, just at the end of the car park for **Wainwright's** pub. This takes you over the footbridge and back to the start of the walk by the riverside path to **Elterwater**.

Refreshments:
Brambles cafe, Chapel Stile

SHORT WALK 4
Lake Coniston and Brantwood

Start/finish	Coniston village SD303975
Time	2hrs walking (plus time for ferry and house visit)
Distance	4½ miles (7km)
Total ascent	40m (144ft)
Parking	LDNP car park, Tilberthwaite Avenue, Coniston (pay and display)
Buses	Services 505/506 from Yewdale Road, Coniston, for Ambleside
Refreshments	Cafes and pubs in Coniston Jumping Jenny's cafe at Brantwood
Maps	OS 1:25,000 OL6, Harvey Superwalker South West sheet

It's worth devoting a whole day to this one. The walking element is no more than a two-hour potter through the lakeshore woodlands, but combined with a trip on the Coniston launch, a tour of Brantwood (and perhaps lunch) and return on the *Gondola*, an entire day can be filled with ease. There is enough to occupy the mind and divert the senses from sore feet – just the thing for a day off from a long-distance walk! Times for the Coniston launch can be obtained from the office on (015394) 36216, and for the steam yacht *Gondola* on (015394) 63856. Note, as the *Gondola* is a National Trust enterprise activity, NT members still have to pay.

The route takes you on a walk down the western bank of Coniston Water from the village, as far as Sunny Bank jetty. From here, a hop on the electric launch takes you to Brantwood, home of John Ruskin from 1872 until his death in 1900. Allow one to three hours here, as there's a lot to see – as well as the house itself, on a fine day you may want some time to explore Ruskin's gardens, which are extensive. When done at Brantwood, catch the steam yacht *Gondola* to chug back to the village in true Victorian style.

If you find yourself in Coniston having had to abandon other walking plans due to bad weather, the trip to Brantwood on the *Gondola* is still a good option, even if you walk only as far as Torver landing stage – or not at all! You can continue the story of Ruskin and Coniston at the excellent Ruskin Museum in the village. This is worth a visit rain or shine for its exhibitions on Lakeland life, the *Bluebird* story and, of course, Ruskin himself.

WHO WAS RUSKIN?

A man difficult to categorize, John Ruskin was born in 1819, the same year as Queen Victoria. Anything but the stereotypical Victorian, he was a man seemingly a century ahead of his peers. Of independent means, he was able to devote his life to art, nature, social reform and high-minded philosophical ideas. Regarded in his lifetime as the country's foremost expert in art and architecture, he also had an unusually perceptive view of nature and the world around him, expressed through his numerous books and paintings. A true visionary, his influence and social ideals were more fully realised in the years following his death at the turn of the century, the new post-empire order owing much to his groundwork.

Ruskin was the first to speak out on a number of social issues that were later addressed in the 20th century by institutions such as the National Trust as well as by government (from the Rent Restriction Act to the creation of smokeless zones). His views on education and emancipation influenced great leaders such as Mahatma Gandhi, but on a more local level he did much to champion the cause of ordinary working people in the north of England – in the late 19th century he supported the setting up of reading rooms in numerous villages in towns, where mill workers and farm labourers could educate themselves or gather to play billiards. Also part of the Arts and Crafts movement, he encouraged the resurgence of the cottage industries of linen and lace-making in Coniston.

From the **car park** by the National Park Information Centre in Coniston, head up towards the centre of the

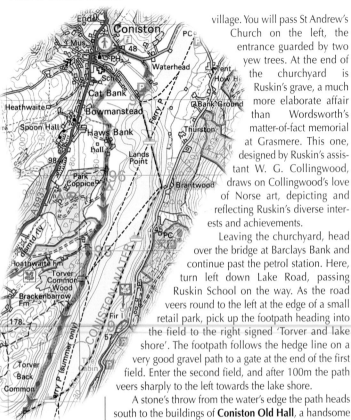

village. You will pass St Andrew's Church on the left, the entrance guarded by two yew trees. At the end of the churchyard is Ruskin's grave, a much more elaborate affair than Wordsworth's matter-of-fact memorial at Grasmere. This one, designed by Ruskin's assistant W. G. Collingwood, draws on Collingwood's love of Norse art, depicting and reflecting Ruskin's diverse interests and achievements.

Leaving the churchyard, head over the bridge at Barclays Bank and continue past the petrol station. Here, turn left down Lake Road, passing Ruskin School on the way. As the road veers round to the left at the edge of a small retail park, pick up the footpath heading into the field to the right signed 'Torver and lake shore'. The footpath follows the hedge line on a very good gravel path to a gate at the end of the first field. Enter the second field, and after 100m the path veers sharply to the left towards the lake shore.

A stone's throw from the water's edge the path heads south to the buildings of **Coniston Old Hall**, a handsome 16th-century affair with distinctive circular chimneys. From the approach to the Old Hall, if you look across the lake you may spot the orange walls of Brantwood – the home of Ruskin. Entering the grounds of Coniston Old Hall by the tarred lane, you may be surprised to discover the grand building functions as … a campsite booking office – but then the property is owned by the National Trust! Continue through to the campsite, where you will see signage indicating the route to Torver through the site.

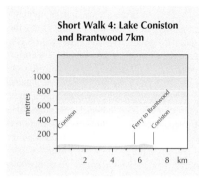

Short Walk 4: Lake Coniston and Brantwood 7km

Brantwood from the launch – the electric launch is an effortless way to complete a circular walk

191

Coming to the end of the camping area, the path leaves the tarmac to join a gravel track heading leftwards to the lake shore. When you meet a National Trust sign to Torver pointing away from the lake, ignore this and keep to the lakeside. A few minutes after this you are directed around the back of a small lakeside plantation before heading down to a boathouse by a water sports centre.

Here you join the lakeside once more, entering Torver Commons, an area of dappled oak woodlands and birdsong. As there is no road on the western edge of Coniston, from this point in the walk you can expect peace and quiet, sharing the route with fellow ramblers on the Cumbrian Way. The small oak trees give way to conifers and beech as you splash across a beck to the Torver landing stage.

To reach Sunny Bank, continue southwards from this first jetty along the lake shore, ignoring a path signed off to Torver after 100m. From here the lakeshore path is straightforward and easy to follow.

WOODLAND INDUSTRY

You will see that much of the woodland around Coniston comprises tall, quite spindly trees, sprouting in bunches from the base. These are old coppice woodlands. Also dotted about these woods, but less obvious, are old bloomeries – where iron ore was smelted, using charcoal made in the woods from coppiced poles. Although iron ore is heavy, the sheer volume of wood needed to make the charcoal to smelt it meant that iron ore was usually transported to the woodlands for smelting rather than the other way round.

Leaving Torver woodland briefly, you enter more open fellside of gorse and bracken reaching down to the lake shore. Some easier walking through an interesting mixture of hollies, juniper, gorse and broadleaves eventually brings you down to **Sunny Bank jetty**. The Coniston launch leaves here several times a day for Brantwood, and times are posted on the jetty. The quiet launch runs on an electric motor, and the battery is topped up by solar panels mounted on the cabin roof.

BRANTWOOD

A modest cottage when Ruskin first bought it unseen from an acquaintance in 1872, Brantwood soon gained a round tower to afford the artist uninterrupted views of the lake from his bedroom. Later additions to the building and grounds saw the 18th-century cottage transformed into a 250 acre estate by Ruskin's death in 1900. Today the house and gardens are managed by the Brantwood Trust, and open to the public daily from mid-March to mid-November. Details from www.brantwood.org.uk or (015394) 41396. ▶

Refreshments:
Jumping Jenny cafe, Brantwood

Head through the lower gardens to catch the steam yacht *Gondola* from the **jetty**, and get off at Coniston landing. From here, head 200m towards the head of the lake and cross a footbridge to reach a footpath leading to the Hawkshead road. Follow this into **Coniston** village, back to your starting point on the left.

Brantwood House, former home of John Ruskin

SHORT WALK 5
Muncaster Fell and Ravenglass
from the Eskdale railway

Start	Irton Road station SD137999
Finish	Ravenglass station SD085965
Time	2½hrs
Distance	6 miles (9.5km)
Total ascent	255m (830ft)
Parking	Parking at Irton Road and Ravenglass stations
Refreshments	Cafe and pubs in Ravenglass
Maps	OS 1:25,000 OL6, Harvey Superwalker South West sheet

This is an unusual outing, taking advantage of the unique 'Ratty' railway to make a linear walk into a circular trip. Having explored something of middle Eskdale in Stage 5, this takes things to a natural conclusion, climbing an outlying Lakeland fell before descending to the sea at Ravenglass – to return under steam. A little bit of planning will be required before setting out to ensure you catch the train back. Train services run through most of the year, but are more frequent in summer – as a rough guide you can expect a service at least hourly between March and October. Details are posted at the stations or contact the railway direct on (01229) 717171, www.ravenglass-railway.co.uk.

You may prefer to start your walk at Eskdale Green rather than Irton Road if this is closer to your accommodation. If so simply take the bridleway by Bankend Wood to join the Muncaster bridleway connecting to the Muncaster fell path.

Wainwright in his wonderful handwritten booklet *Walks from Ratty* describes a similar walk, and recommends walking it towards Irton Road to get the views of the fells. You decide – other than a personal preference to walk towards the coast, a certain amount of pragmatism leads me to contradict the great man's advice. You'll see fewer people walking towards the sea, and, having completed the route, you can fill in the rest of your day in Ravenglass as you wish – there's the railway museum, Muncaster Castle with its owl sanctuary and gardens, and two pubs where you can grab an evening meal as the sun hits the western horizon.

Eskdale railway, or 'Ratty' as it is affectionately known, carries passengers between the sea and the hills

Irton Road station, the starting point, is a great spot for snapping photos of the steam engines pulling their miniature passenger trains through the fell country. You don't need to be a train spotter to feel something of the magic of this particular scene. Leaving the station to start your walk, pause on the bridge above the tracks – if you've timed it well you will have the Eskdale fells as the backdrop and the picturesque sight of a steam locomotive in the foreground. Continue along the tarred lane past the group of cottages at Hollerstones, after 100m, and past the aptly named Mountain View cottage. It's a lovely old lane with wavy dry-stone walls struggling to stand up, bordered by gorse and daffodils in the spring.

195

At Forest How the bridleway becomes a grassy lane by the side of the property – you feel as though you are walking through someone's garden – before continuing through a metal gate into the gorse beyond. Carry on, ignoring a footpath to the left 75m or so from the gate. After a further 200m, take the footpath to the right as you meet the corner of a

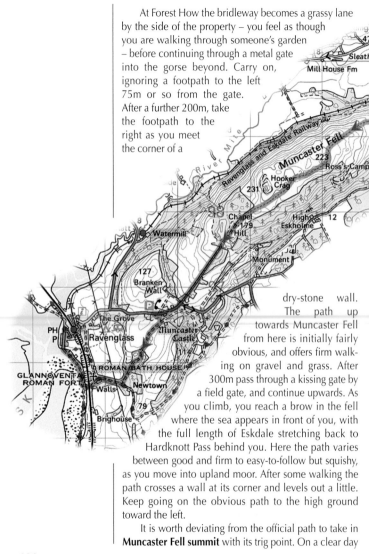

dry-stone wall. The path up towards Muncaster Fell from here is initially fairly obvious, and offers firm walking on gravel and grass. After 300m pass through a kissing gate by a field gate, and continue upwards. As you climb, you reach a brow in the fell where the sea appears in front of you, with the full length of Eskdale stretching back to Hardknott Pass behind you. Here the path varies between good and firm to easy-to-follow but squishy, as you move into upland moor. After some walking the path crosses a wall at its corner and levels out a little. Keep going on the obvious path to the high ground toward the left.

It is worth deviating from the official path to take in **Muncaster Fell summit** with its trig point. On a clear day

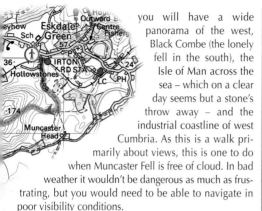

you will have a wide panorama of the west, Black Combe (the lonely fell in the south), the Isle of Man across the sea – which on a clear day seems but a stone's throw away – and the industrial coastline of west Cumbria. As this is a walk primarily about views, this is one to do when Muncaster Fell is free of cloud. In bad weather it wouldn't be dangerous as much as frustrating, but you would need to be able to navigate in poor visibility conditions.

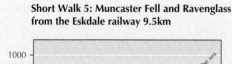

ROMAN RAVENGLASS

The summit of Muncaster Fell is likely to have been a signalling station in Roman times. The historian Robin Collingwood surmised that from here messages could be relayed from Ravenglass to Ambleside in a matter of minutes, using a chain of hilltop fire beacons.

Collingwood (son of W. G. Collingwood, writer and antiquarian) also identified the Roman ruins at Walls Castle, passed later on the walk, to be those of a

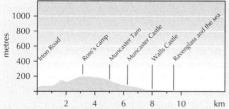

Short Walk 5: Muncaster Fell and Ravenglass from the Eskdale railway 9.5km

Roman bath house. The walls of the bath house still stand, remarkably well preserved and four metres high, now under the guardianship of English Heritage and open to the public. Although modest, they have been described as amongst the best Roman remains, and are well worth a visit if train times permit.

Why the bath house and nearby fort were built is uncertain. Perhaps it was in preparation for an attack on Ireland, or as an extension of Hadrian's defences down the western coast from Carlisle. Certainly it would have been an important supply post for the northern garrisons. See www.english-heritage.org.uk.

Ravenglass was certainly an important site in Hadrian's day, the western terminus of Lakeland's main Roman road, linking the sea to the heart of the Lake District at Ambleside. Nothing can be seen of this ancient route today, though it is assumed that it followed the valley floor through Eskdale en route to Hardknott fort.

From the trig point at the top of the fell, head down the fell's southern flank to pick up the footpath heading southwest and seaward between two stands of conifers. The path skirts the left-hand edge of the most northerly plantation. Reaching the end of the conifers you will see a kissing gate amidst some rhododendrons. Go through here and continue downhill, passing **Muncaster Tarn** on your right. Where a bridleway goes off to the left here, keep on the main bridleway signed to Muncaster. Soon another track will join yours from the right; keep straight on here. Your way soon runs on to a very straight section of road, heading down to the sea – the sands of Ravenglass stretch out in front of you.

Reaching the main road at a corner, head downhill for 300m, passing Muncaster Country Guest House to reach the grand entrance to **Muncaster Castle** on the left. Go through here, following the walkers' and cyclists' permitted route off to the right at the first building you meet. The permitted path soon reaches a gate, from where it becomes a track, then a public footpath. It's a very pleasant stroll through the grounds of the Muncaster estate on this track – the woodlands pungent with wild garlic.

MUNCASTER CASTLE

This, along with the Roman bath house nearby, makes an interesting diversion before heading into Ravenglass village, although if you want to explore the medieval building as well as its grounds you may need more than a couple of hours. In the spring and the autumn, it's the gardens at Muncaster Castle that draw the crowds. Muncaster is famed for its azaleas – quite a sight when all in flower. There's also an owl centre and cafe here. The grounds are open year round, for a charge – for information tel (01229) 717614 or visit www.muncastercastle.co.uk.

Emerging from the woodlands at a junction of tracks opposite a white house, take the public footpath heading down the track to the right, away from the buildings. After passing Walls garden cottage (Walls a reference to the Roman heritage here) turn left at the junction to follow a lane in front of some grand houses. The footpath ducks under the railway line to come out onto the beach below Ravenglass village. Head along the sands to the end of the road, and walk down pretty main street in **Ravenglass**. Find the Old Butcher's Craft and Gift Shop off to the right-hand side of the main street – the lane to the side of this brings you into a car park area by the Ratty Arms hotel. From here, a footbridge brings you to the platform to join the train.

SHORT WALK 6
Scale Force and Crummock
from Buttermere village

Start/finish	Bridge Hotel, Buttermere NY174169
Time	2hrs
Distance	4½ miles (7.5km)
Total ascent	220m (720ft)
Parking	Long How, NY173172, NT, pay and display
	Buttermere, NY174169, LDNP, pay and display
Buses/ferry	Seasonal Honister Rambler (77) from Keswick
Refreshments	Hotels and cafe in Buttermere
Maps	OS 1:25,000 OL4, Harvey Superwalker West sheet

The objective of this short walk is Scale Force, hidden away in a ravine two miles from Buttermere village. An easy evening stroll for the fell walker, Scale Force's distance from Buttermere puts it beyond the reach of the picnic-by-the-car brigade, so it's usually a quiet spot, sometimes visited by walkers coming down off Red Pike above.

It's very much a walk between views, starting with the tranquil woods and waters of Crummock and leading to the crags and cascades at Scale Force. With a vertical drop of 52m (172ft), Scale Force can claim to be Lakeland's longest waterfall. The best views of the falling waters are from below, although the tangle of rock by the base of the falls makes it difficult to get up really close to fully appreciate the drop. The best vantage point is a few metres away just above the bridge.

From the Bridge Hotel in **Buttermere** head initially towards Buttermere lake, picking up a gravel bridleway signed 'Buttermere Lake and Scale Bridge' just to the left of Buttermere's second hostelry, the Fish Hotel. There must be one pub for every three inhabitants of this small village! After 50m the bridleway turns 90° to the left, and after a further 50m it turns 90° to the right. At this point

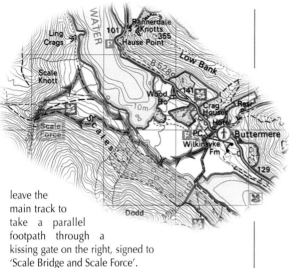

leave the main track to take a parallel footpath through a kissing gate on the right, signed to 'Scale Bridge and Scale Force'.

Today's Buttermere and Crummock Water lakes originally formed one large expanse of water, filling an area carved out by the retreating glacier that formed the catchment area of the River Cocker. River deposits, washed down in the millennia since, have choked up the shallows here to form an alluvial plain, thus creating two lakes. So, between the two lakes, we now walk on what once would have been water!

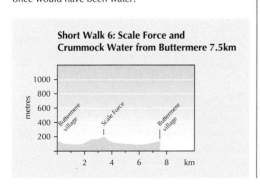

Short Walk 6: Scale Force and Crummock Water from Buttermere 7.5km

A solid farm double-track leads to **Scale Bridge** – a curious looking thing with two arches. Go through the gate at the far side of the bridge and head right to walk through some old woodland on an obvious, well-used path. There are views back over Buttermere village, with Newlands valley behind. Crummock Water creeps into the foreground, with Whiteless Pike and Rannerdale Knotts on the far bank. Behind these, the rugged heights of Grasmoor fill the background to the left.

It's a firm and level path initially. Above Crummock Water, when you come close to the Holme Islands just offshore, the path splits – take the left-hand option, after

Crummock Water, as seen from the footpath to Scale Force

50m crossing Far Ruddy Beck by a narrow wooden **squeeze bridge**. From here the path starts to lead away from the lake shore, heading uphill, the trees thinning out to leave just the odd hawthorn and holly. Now moving diagonally up the fellside through bracken, head into the obvious ravine above. From this open fellside here you really feel like a Lord in his realm, with tremendous views over the lush Buttermere valley and lake. The path is indistinct at times, but just head up into the gully, the going getting progressively more marshy as you climb into an area of upland bog.

Eventually you reach a dry-stone wall with a kissing gate, leading down to a footbridge just under **Scale Force**. Climb up as far as you dare. The lower section of the waterfall is obscured by a rocky outcrop – there used to be an iron handrail, but no more!

To continue, return to the footbridge at the base of the falls, cross over and turn right, downhill, to pass through an iron gate 30m from the bridge. The footpath now follows the beck downhill towards the lake, through gorse bushes and over another little footbridge (this one going over Black Beck). Continue through more gorse by the beck side to reach a beautifully crafted round **sheepfold** right by the side of the path. A small wooden footbridge, 50m beyond the sheepfold, takes you over the beck. Go through the gate at the far side, and head back in the direction of Buttermere over a second narrow footbridge.

From here the path gets a bit boggy and vague, but all branches of the path come together at the lakeside by Scale Island. A now obvious gravel path rejoins the path you walked earlier at Far Ruddy Beck, 20m downhill from the squeeze footbridge by some dilapidated sheepfolds. Retrace your steps to **Scale Bridge**, and cross to return to the start of the walk.

SHORT WALK 7
The Borrowdale Yews
from Rosthwaite

Start/finish	Royal Oak Hotel, Rosthwaite, NY258148
Time	2½hrs
Distance	5 miles (8.5km)
Total ascent	165m (540ft)
Parking	Rosthwaite, NY257148, NT, Pay and Display
Buses/ferry	Regular Borrowdale Rambler (79) from Keswick
Refreshments	Hotels and cafe in Rosthwaite
	Cafe in Seatoller
Maps	OS 1:25,000 OL4, Harvey Superwalker West sheet

This is an ideal afternoon or summer evening stroll, with plenty of interest. Starting amidst the lanes and cottages of Rosthwaite, it leads into the languid riverside meadows of Longthwaite before heading up to the old graphite mining area of Seathwaite. Its Klondike period now long since passed, Seathwaite is now a peaceful Lakeland backwater, most usually passed by walkers heading up to Scafell or the surrounding peaks. The walk has something for everyone – waterfalls, woodlands, a little bit of history – and for very little exertion!

You might want to revisit the Royal Oak or the neighbouring Scafell Hotel later for sustenance, but for now ... on with the walk!

Start your walk from the Royal Oak hotel in **Rosthwaite**, 50m down the road from the post office. ◄ On the opposite side of the Borrowdale road from the hotels a footpath takes you down a tarred lane, weaving between the houses, and soon becomes a rougher cobbled track. As the tarmac returns underfoot, just behind Yew Tree Farm (you will see the Flock Inn cafe in the gaps between the houses), keep left to pass **Nook Farm** on your right.

At a green, tin-roofed building turn right, and after 10m turn left onto a signed footpath through a gate into a field. Follow the left boundary to the bottom of the

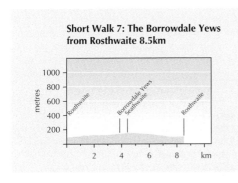

**Short Walk 7: The Borrowdale Yews
from Rosthwaite 8.5km**

field to go over a wooden stile built into the wall.
Entering the next field, follow the path as it veers rightward to go through a hole in the wall on the right-hand
side. Now head leftward to go through a field gate at the
end of this third field and reach a tarred lane by some
white cottages.

At the cottages turn right, downhill, to cross
the stone bridge over the Derwent to take
the footpath leading though the grounds
of Borrowdale Youth Hostel to the
left. The footpath passes the front
door of the timber-clad hostel
and continues on to a good
gravel path by the side of the
Derwent. A kissing gate
200m from the hostel
leads into some river-
side hazel wood-
land. For 30m
there is a

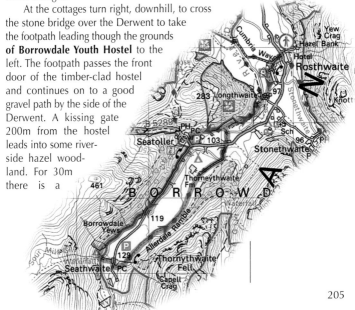

straightforward but careful scramble over some greasy rocks under the trees, before a kissing gate brings you out onto an easier gravel footpath. From here the footpath, bordered to the left with a dry-stone wall, heads away from the river very gently uphill through mossy woodland.

Leaving the woodlands around **Longthwaite** via another kissing gate the path levels out, in bracken and rough grazing, and traces a wall on the left before ducking through a hole in the wall at the end of the field. You will see **Folly Bridge** below to the left, but instead of heading down to it, keep right and climb slightly uphill into more woodland with some notably large holly trees.

As the path continues through a hole in the wall, some great views of the fells around Stonethwaite open up to the left. Less appealingly, some sewage works hide in the woodland below. Here ignore a path through the wall to the right, and instead keep to the larger main track through the trees towards another larger timber-clad building (a hotel) visible ahead. Approaching the hotel, the path ducks through the wall to the right, then turns leftwards to splash over a beck to follow a wall

Rosthwaite Bridge, with the village of Rosthwaite beyond

down to the outskirts of **Seatoller**. A small group of stately Scots pines stands by the edge of the National Trust car park, from where you meet the Seatoller road.

On reaching the road by the bus stop, turn right if you want to seek a bite to eat at the Yew Tree cafe ▶ or if you want to visit the National Park Information Centre in the village. Otherwise turn left for 100m and reach the road junction with an old-style black-and-white finger post. Take the road signed 'Seathwaite and Styhead Pass' to the right, which heads over Seatoller bridge. Glaramara is the prominent peak at the end of the valley to the left, with Bowfell in the far distance. You will pass a small campsite on the left-hand side of the road.

From Seatoller there's a 1km stretch of tarmac bashing, albeit on a usually quiet road. About halfway along you will see a little stone bridge marooned in a field to the left. Continue on to reach the sturdy **Seathwaite bridge** that takes the road over the beck. Here at Seathwaite bridge take the footpath signed to Seathwaite to the right, along a grassy track by the river bank. Ahead in the distance, the white streaks of Sour Milk Gill cascade down the fellside from Gillercomb. The track skirts past sparse scrub woodland, scrabbling for a foothold on the fell to the right. These fells were exploited for their graphite in times past, but more on this later. At the end of this scrub, by the riverside you will meet a large distinctive yew tree, one of three that make up the collection known as the Borrowdale Yews.

Refreshments:
Yew Tree cafe, Seatoller. A charming wayside eatery, housed in an old house in the heart of the village.

THE BORROWDALE YEWS AND BLACK LEAD

The only Lakeland trees to be named on the Ordnance Survey maps, the Borrowdale Yews have a myth associated with them. The legend goes that one of the trees, uprooted in a winter storm, revealed its black treasure beneath – graphite. True or otherwise, the mining of graphite (plumbago, or black lead, as it is also known) brought great wealth to the area for a time. This rare mineral, originally used locally for marking sheep, was mined commercially for 300 years from the 16th century, and most famously turned into pencils at the Keswick factories.

The Seathwaite mines were for many years the only source of graphite in mainland Europe, and thus graphite was more sought after than gold or copper. Prices for graphite reached an incredible peak of nearly £4000 per ton – and this back in the early 19th century! Such was the scarcity and value of the commodity that miners were routinely strip-searched on leaving the mines in a vain attempt to combat theft – yet illicit trade and smuggling were rife.

Ultimately graphite finds abroad and technological improvements at home (whereby less pure graphite could be combined with kaolin to make pencil leads) caused the price to crash. The strung-out workings of the Seathwaite valley were abandoned by the beginning of the 20th century – the glory days long gone. If you visit the valley before the summer bracken covers them, you may see the old spoil heaps dotted about the fellside above Seathwaite.

Continue through the kissing gate to the right of the large yew, with Sour Milk Gill to the right grabbing your attention. From here it's a pleasant riverside amble along a gently undulating path. Bizarrely, you pass over the gravestone of a John Banks just before the point where Sour Milk Gill meets the main beck. Cross over the Sour Milk **footbridge**, then over the **footbridge** spanning the main beck (the Derwent here is no more than a beck!) to enter a walled lane leading into the farm buildings at Seathwaite.

As you come into **Seathwaite**, turn right up the cobbles, reaching a wooden fingerpost a few metres beyond the farm buildings. Take the footpath signed 'Thorneythwaite' off to the left here, over a sleeper bridge, and go through a field gate onto a gravel track with a wall to the left-hand side. After 120m go through a kissing gate into the field on the left, and a few cairns guide you on your way through the middle of the field. ◀ The path comes in to meet the wall at the bottom left-

Seathwaite lives up to its rainy reputation here – it's very boggy!

Sour Milk Gill – near the rainiest place in England

hand corner of the field. Continue through several fields. The path becomes a well-defined single track, winding its way down the valley through kissing gates, following the walls. After a while the path widens to double track, which passes through several gated fields.

The footpath heads off to the right by **Thorneythwaite Farm**, clearly signed, and shortly meets the farm's access lane. Turn right on this rough tarred lane, following it to the main Borrowdale road at **Strands Bridge**. Cross over the road here to pick up a footpath by the bridge signed to Longthwaite. This path follows the river for 150m to cross the river again by **Folly Bridge**, then heads diagonally uphill to the right to rejoin the path you took earlier back to **Borrowdale Youth Hostel**. Once at the hostel, follow the tarred lane back over the bridge, turning left at the white houses at the corner to retrace your steps back to **Rosthwaite**. ▶

Refreshments: the menu of the Flock Inn cafe draws heavily on the Herdwick sheep farming of the area, and is a prime example of an enterprising farming family diversifying their business. Try a 'Herdiburger' for example!

SHORT WALK 8
Wordworth's Grasmere and Rydal via Loughrigg Terrace

Start/finish	Grasmere church, NY337073
Time	Allow 3½hrs, plus extra time if visiting the museums
Distance	6½ miles (11km)
Total ascent	330m (1090ft)
Parking	White Moss Common, NY350065, NT pay and display
	Grasmere village, NY339072, LDNP pay and display
	Pelter Bridge, NY365059, LDNP free (but small)
Buses	Grasmere, Dove Cottage and Rydal are on the 555 route
Refreshments	Grasmere village, Dove Cottage, Rydal Mount
Maps	OS 1:25,000 OL7, Harvey Superwalker Central sheet

This half-day walk is easily extended to a leisurely day if you wish to explore the Wordsworth connections – the route passes by both Dove Cottage and Rydal Mount, two former homes of the great poet who composed some of his best-known lines while in residence. Even without the Wordsworth associations, this is truly a classic Lakeland low-level walk. The scenery is spectacular at any time of the year and the going is easy.

However, all things come with a price, and the penalty for enjoying all this walk has to offer is the company of numerous others, for this is a very popular walk. If solitude is called for, plan on starting either very early or very late in the day. Sunrise and sunset also add a little more magic, if some were needed, to the lake scenes.

If you are not walking the Tour, and thus not bound to start this walk from Grasmere itself, you may prefer to park at White Moss Common and pick up the route from this point instead.

Your starting point is the church in the centre of **Grasmere** – its graveyard the last resting point of William Wordsworth. It's a very picturesque spot, although you

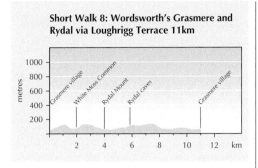

Short Walk 8: Wordsworth's Grasmere and Rydal via Loughrigg Terrace 11km

may be underwhelmed by the ordinariness of Wordsworth's gravestone itself! From the church head out along the road in the Ambleside direction, passing the Rowan Tree restaurant and a large national park car park on the edge of the village. In front of you on the main road you will see the round slate building housing the Wordsworth Trust's latest development – cross over the main road to reach it. This is the Jerwood Building, a rare example of contemporary architecture within the national park. From its office you can pick up tickets for the museum next door, the 3 Degrees West Gallery just over the road and Dove Cottage itself.

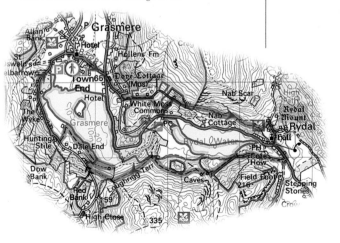

DOVE COTTAGE

Home of the poet and his sister, Dorothy, from 1799 to 1808, Dove Cottage is open 9.30am–5.30pm daily, closed mid-January to mid February. For further details telephone the Wordsworth Trust on (015394) 35544 or visit www.wordsworth.org.uk.

Continue 30m from the Jerwood Building to pass **Dove Cottage** on the left, or dodge between the buildings for refreshments at the Dove Cottage tea rooms by the main road. To continue with the walk, carry on along the little road by Dove Cottage, heading slightly uphill. Towards the top of the brow, on the left-hand side of the lane, is a 'coffin stone'. This is a hangover from earlier times when, for want of consecrated burial ground in Ambleside, coffins had to be carried the four miles from Ambleside to Grasmere along the corpse road we now follow in the opposite direction as far as Rydal. This coffin stone was used to rest the heavy load while the bearers got their breath back.

Ignore the first footpath 5m from the coffin stone and continue upwards, past a pond, to a black-and-white signpost at a road junction. Follow the 'no through road' up the hill to the left, ignoring a signpost a little further up for Alcock Tarn. The road starts to level out by some marshland to the left, and here you pick up a bridleway to the right signed to Whitemoss car park. This brings you down a gravel track through the trees to the main road by the smaller car park at Whitemoss Common. Cross over the road and work your way along the paths in the trees leftwards to reach the main National Trust car park at **White Moss**. ◀

This is an alternative starting point for the walk.

From the main car park entrance, turn left along the main road to Grasmere for 100m. By a red post box on the opposite side of the road, pick up a public footpath which leads up a track past **Coach House**, nestled under the crags, and into a woodland with a ghyll splashing its way through the trees. By the first waterfall, 100m from the road you left, take the right-hand branch in the path that steers you onto a track between two walls, and running water replaces the sound of traffic. Ignore a field gate to the right, and continue through the gate in front to climb up to meet a track just under a green house. Here, turn right and contour across the fellside with views of Rydal Water and Loughrigg Fell opening up to your right.

There is a great feeling of space with this walk, and a park-like quality to the landscape; the substantial oak trees in the near ground are spaced sufficiently so as not to obscure the view beyond. After a few hundred metres of walking along this well-defined path with a dry-stone wall to the right-hand side, Nab Scar looms up from the left. Its craggy profile will be familiar to anyone who has completed the Fairfield Horseshoe – this last fell of the round is a killer on the knees in the descent! Today, though, we just admire it from beneath.

Under Nab Scar the path goes through a small field gate in the wall. Rydal Water here is tantalisingly veiled by the foliage of the trees in the summer. A larger field gate leads out of the woodlands, with the views of Rydal opening up again. The well-defined double-track bridleway continues, crossing some walls on the way, and bracken now replaces the trees on this more open section of fellside. Look out for some particularly old and knarled oak trees along here sprouting mosses, ferns and liverworts. Level with the end of the lake, the path starts to climb very slightly to go through a field gate and into a lonnin, shortly to descend into the hamlet of Rydal Mount. ▶

On reaching the Rydal Mount road that climbs up from the main road below, turn right and go downhill for 50m to reach **Rydal Mount** itself, home of Wordsworth from 1813 to 1850. Continue downhill, passing the entrance to **Rydal Hall**. ▶

It's not just Wordsworth's house that is worthy of note here at Rydal. A lovely church, the old farm buildings and cottages, and the Victorian villas that sprung up to the poet's fury combine to give the place a picture-postcard feel. On reaching the main road, follow the pavement for 250m to the left, before crossing the River Rothay by **Pelter Bridge**.

**Rydal Mount
house and gardens**
Open daily
March–October
9.30am–5.30pm,
November–February
10.00am–4.00pm.
Closed Tuesdays
in winter, and
8th January –
1st February.

Refreshments:
Tea shop at Rydal
Hall on the left.

Rydal Cave

Once over the bridge, pick up the 'no through road' to the right by the riverside, passing the small LDNP car park. Continue along the small tarred lane, past **Cote How** guesthouse to the end of the road at a gate by a row of four sturdy slate terraced houses. From here follow the marked public bridleway, the tarmac giving way to a cobble and gravel lane. As you descend to a second gate, Rydal Water again springs into view. Here there is an option of a bridleway heading down to the lake shore to the right, but instead take the permitted bridlepath straight ahead signed to Loughrigg Terrace via Rydal Cave.

You are walking into a landscape typical of the Borrowdale Volcanic region – a carpet of green thinly covering the rocks, with trees grabbing a tenuous foothold in the shallow soils. As you come across the first cave just to the left of the path it is as if the rocks can no longer contain themselves, and huge angular boulders burst out to the surface. With care, you can peer into the dark realms beneath.

The bridleway continues uphill through the spoil of past mining efforts before levelling out again. To the left are the craggy outcrops of Loughrigg; to the right Rydal Water, with the white splash of Nab Cottage on its far bank and Nab Scar behind. Continue onwards on a gentle downhill gradient. Roughly at the head of Rydal Water the path forks – keep high for the views, splashing across two small streams about 30m from the fork. A few hardy hawthorns, hollies and juniper bushes cling bravely to the side of these ghylls. This really is a section to amble along and enjoy the views.

As you come to the brow of the slope, Grasmere enters the scene. Keep on the fellside path to get the best views, then come to an iron kissing gate. Go through the gate and immediately afterwards onto a footpath to the right through a National Trust labelled gate to Grasmere, and continue downhill on an old cobbled lane. The lane enters rhododendron and mixed woodland, avoiding the sometimes busy and tortuous section of the Red Bank road to Grasmere above. On reaching the house by the Red Bank road, instead of going onto the road turn sharp right at the house and follow the sign back to the lake. When your woodland path meets the lakeshore path turn left and head in the direction of Grasmere village.

The lakeshore path allows you as far as a **boathouse**, at which point you are steered back up to the road. Turn right to follow the road downhill, past some impressive and individual homes, and continue into **Grasmere** village.

Bluebells on the slopes above Grasmere in late May

SHORT WALK 9
Howtown and Ullswater
from Glenridding

Start/finish	Glenridding pier, NY337073
Time	Allow 4hrs, including steamer crossing
Distance	6½ miles (10.5km)
Total ascent	330m (1110ft)
Parking	Glenridding pier, NY389169
Buses	Infrequent, summer-only service to Windermere
Refreshments	Glenridding and Patterdale villages
Map	OS 1:25,000 OL5

A real classic Lakeland low-level route – ideal for a relaxing 'day off' from walking the Tour, a wet-weather walk or a family day out with a picnic. The walking is easy, the scenery is superb, and the trip on the Ullswater steamer is not to be missed either. Starting from Glenridding pier, a 35 minute boat trip takes you to Howtown, midway down Ullswater. From here a mainly level walk on good paths leads through lakeshore woodlands with picture-postcard views all the way back to your starting point.

The problem? Well, you won't be the first to have had this great idea for a day out. On a summer weekend, you will be far from alone when you get off the steamer at Howtown – but persevere, the crowds will thin out within a few hundred metres of the jetty. Find yourself a quiet spot by the lake for a picnic (you will be spoilt for choice), relax, and amble your way back to Glenridding at a pace that suits. If you can, time your trip for mid-week, out of school holidays – but if this is not possible, don't despair. This may be the busiest route described in this guidebook, but its popularity is deserved.

The natural grandeur of the lake is complemented by the Victorian-style public transport. Steamers have been taking tourists to Howtown from Glenridding since 1859, although *Raven* and *Lady of the Lake* were converted to diesel in the 1930s. In high season steamer services are hourly, while out of the summer months a less frequent service operates. For details, tel: (017684) 82229.

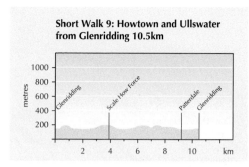

Short Walk 9: Howtown and Ullswater from Glenridding 10.5km

From the end of the **Howtown jetty**, take the public footpath signed to Sandwick on the right, over the footbridge. After 200m the gravel track leads to a tarred lane. Head right towards the lake shore here, picking up a footpath to the left after 100m. The path now heads up through the fields and trees to reach a kissing gate. Turn right here and head once more towards the lake shore, having gained some height above the bay. From here you will get views back over to Howtown and see the steamer departing for its next stop, Pooley Bridge.

Now on a distinct, well-used path amidst the bracken, you will find yourself on some small cliffs above Ullswater, walking almost at treetop level above the oak trees anchored by the water's edge. The bracken-covered slopes of Hallin Fell over to the left now give

The steamer leaving Howtown, the start of the easy walk by Ullswater's shore

217

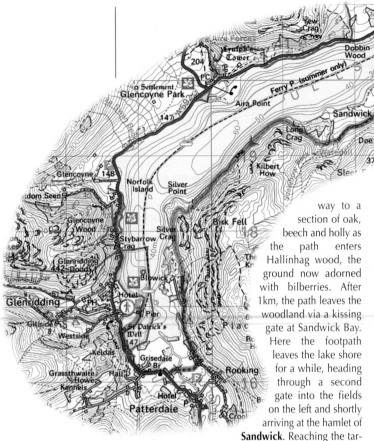

way to a section of oak, beech and holly as the path enters Hallinhag wood, the ground now adorned with bilberries. After 1km, the path leaves the woodland via a kissing gate at Sandwick Bay. Here the footpath leaves the lake shore for a while, heading through a second gate into the fields on the left and shortly arriving at the hamlet of **Sandwick**. Reaching the tarmac road at Sandwick, head uphill for 100m, before taking a public bridleway off to the right.

The bridleway from Sandwick stays away from the lake for the time being, contouring round the lower slopes of Sleet Fell, but affords great views back over the water. As you cross a footbridge, just as the path turns lakewards once more, look out for **Scalehow Force** – a waterfall easily missed on the fellside above to the left.

Returning to the lake shore, the path continues close by Ullswater for several kilometres, passing through charming open woodlands, over rocky outcrops perched above the lake and by quiet shaded shingle beaches. No directions are necessary – this is a walk to savour and amble along on a summer's afternoon.

Approaching the head of the lake, Glenridding landing stage – the start of the walk – comes into view, and the valleys of Grisedale and Glenridding beyond. Dollywagon Pike can be seen between at the head of Grisdale; St Sunday Crag the more prominent peak in the foreground behind Patterdale village. Eventually the bridleway you have been following passes **Side Farm** campsite at the head of the lake. Continue to the farm buildings, where you turn right and follow the access lane back to the main road at **Patterdale**. Now turn right to return to Glenridding landing stage – there are pavements or permissive paths by the roadside all the way.

Patterdale village

APPENDIX 1
Useful contacts

Lake District Weatherline	(0870) 550 575
	www.lake-district.gov.uk/weatherline
Cumbria Tourist Board	(015394) 44444
	www.golakes.co.uk
Youth Hostel Association	(0870) 770 8868
	www.yha.org.uk
Lake District National Park	www.lake-district.gov.uk
The National Trust	www.nationaltrust.org.uk
The Ramblers' Association	www.ramblers.co.uk
Friends of the Lake District	www.fld.org.uk

APPENDIX 2
Tourist Information Centres

The Tourist Information Centres passed on the Tour are listed below. Please note, some of the smaller offices may be closed out of the main season.

Ambleside	(015394) 32582
	www.amblesideonline.co.uk
Windermere	(015394) 46491
	www.golakes.co.uk
Coniston	(015394) 41533
Keswick	(017687) 72645
	www.keswick.org
Ullswater	(017684) 82414

For planning a walking tour or arranging accommodation, Kendal Tourist Information Centre is well placed to help, and is open all year round (tel. 01539 725758).

APPENDIX 3
Transport information

Buses
The best source of information is the online timetables available from the transport section of www.cumbria.gov.uk

Alternatively call the Traveline on (0870) 608 2608 or pick up a bus timetable when in the Lake District from any library, tourist information office or bus.

Trains
On the internet, information on timetables may be obtained from www.nationalrail.co.uk or www.thetrainline.com, where you can purchase tickets on line.

The National Rail enquiries telephone number is (08457) 48 49 50.

APPENDIX 4
Selected bibliography

Recommended reading
The Rough Guide to the Lake District, Jules Brown, Rough Guides, London

A Walk Around the Lakes, Hunter Davies, Orion, London

Guide to the Lakes, William Wordsworth, OUP, Oxford

Portrait of the Lakes, and other titles, Norman Nicholson, Robert Hale, London

Background reading on Lakeland history
At Lakeland's Heart, John Masson Carnie, Parrock Press, Windermere

The English Lakes – The Hills, The People, Their History, Ramshaw and Adams, P3 Publications

Lakeland Valleys, Robert Gambles, Heritage Guides, Devon (o/p)

The Lake District, Milward and Robinson, Methuen, London

The Making of the English Landscape, W. G. Hoskins, Penguin, London

The History of the Countryside, Oliver Rackham, Dent Publications, London

Keswick – the Story of a Lake District Town, George Bott, Cumbria County Library, Kendal

LISTING OF CICERONE GUIDES

The Great Glen Way
The Pentland Hills: A Walker's Guide
The Southern Upland Way

IRELAND
The Mountains of Ireland
Irish Coastal Walks
The Irish Coast to Coast

INTERNATIONAL CYCLE GUIDES
The Way of St James – Le Puy to
    Santiago cyclist's guide
The Danube Cycle Way
Cycle Tours in Spain
Cycling the River Loire – The Way
    of St Martin
Cycle Touring in France
Cycling in the French Alps

WALKING AND TREKKING
IN THE ALPS
Tour of Monte Rosa
Walking in the Alps (all Alpine areas)
100 Hut Walks in the Alps
Chamonix to Zermatt
Tour of Mont Blanc
Alpine Ski Mountaineering
    Vol 1 Western Alps
Alpine Ski Mountaineering
    Vol 2 Eastern Alps
Snowshoeing: Techniques and Routes
    in the Western Alps
Alpine Points of View
Tour of the Matterhorn
Across the Eastern Alps: E5

FRANCE, BELGIUM AND
LUXEMBOURG
RLS (Robert Louis Stevenson) Trail
Walks in Volcano Country
French Rock
Walking the French Gorges
Rock Climbs Belgium & Luxembourg
Tour of the Oisans: GR54
Walking in the Tarentaise and
    Beaufortain Alps
Walking in the Haute Savoie, vol. 1
Walking in the Haute Savoie, vol. 2
Tour of the Vanoise
GR20 Corsica – The High Level Route
The Ecrins National Park
Walking the French Alps: GR5
Walking in the Cevennes
Vanoise Ski Touring
Walking in Provence
Walking on Corsica
Mont Blanc Walks
Walking in the Cathar region
    of south west France
Walking in the Dordogne
Trekking in the Vosges and Jura
The Cathar Way

PYRENEES AND FRANCE / SPAIN
Rock Climbs in the Pyrenees
Walks & Climbs in the Pyrenees
The GR10 Trail: Through the
    French Pyrenees

The Way of St James –
    Le Puy to the Pyrenees
The Way of St James –
    Pyrenees-Santiago-Finisterre
Through the Spanish Pyrenees GR11
The Pyrenees – World's Mountain
    Range Guide
The Pyrenean Haute Route
The Mountains of Andorra

SPAIN AND PORTUGAL
Picos de Europa – Walks & Climbs
The Mountains of Central Spain
Walking in Mallorca
Costa Blanca Walks Vol 1
Costa Blanca Walks Vol 2
Walking in Madeira
Via de la Plata (Seville To Santiago)
Walking in the Cordillera Cantabrica
Walking in the Canary Islands 1 West
Walking in the Canary Islands 2 East
Walking in the Sierra Nevada
Walking in the Algarve

SWITZERLAND
Walking in Ticino, Switzerland
Central Switzerland –
    A Walker's Guide
The Bernese Alps
Walking in the Valais
Alpine Pass Route
Walks in the Engadine, Switzerland
Tour of the Jungfrau Region

GERMANY AND AUSTRIA
Klettersteig Scrambles in
    Northern Limestone Alps
King Ludwig Way
Walking in the Salzkammergut
Walking in the Harz Mountains
Germany's Romantic Road
Mountain Walking in Austria
Walking the River Rhine Trail
Trekking in the Stubai Alps
Trekking in the Zillertal Alps

SCANDINAVIA
Walking In Norway
The Pilgrim Road to Nidaros
    (St Olav's Way)

EASTERN EUROPE
The High Tatras
The Mountains of Romania
Walking in Hungary

CROATIA AND SLOVENIA
Walks in the Julian Alps
Walking in Croatia

ITALY
Italian Rock
Walking in the Central Italian Alps
Central Apennines of Italy
Walking in Italy's Gran Paradiso
Long Distance Walks in Italy's Gran
    Paradiso
Walking in Sicily
Shorter Walks in the Dolomites

Treks in the Dolomites
Via Ferratas of the Italian
    Dolomites Vol 1
Via Ferratas of the Italian
    Dolomites Vol 2
Walking in the Dolomites
Walking in Tuscany
Trekking in the Apennines
Through the Italian Alps: the GTA

OTHER MEDITERRANEAN
COUNTRIES
The Mountains of Greece
Climbs & Treks in the Ala Dag
    (Turkey)
The Mountains of Turkey
Treks & Climbs Wadi Rum, Jordan
Jordan – Walks, Treks, Caves etc.
Crete – The White Mountains
Walking in Western Crete
Walking in Malta

AFRICA
Climbing in the Moroccan Anti-Atlas
Trekking in the Atlas Mountains
Kilimanjaro

NORTH AMERICA
The Grand Canyon &
    American South West
Walking in British Columbia
The John Muir Trail

SOUTH AMERICA
Aconcagua

HIMALAYAS – NEPAL, INDIA
Langtang, Gosainkund &
    Helambu: A Trekkers' Guide
Garhwal & Kumaon –
    A Trekkers' Guide
Kangchenjunga – A Trekkers' Guide
Manaslu – A Trekkers' Guide
Everest – A Trekkers' Guide
Annapurna – A Trekker's Guide
Bhutan – A Trekker's Guide

TECHNIQUES AND EDUCATION
The Adventure Alternative
Rope Techniques
Snow & Ice Techniques
Mountain Weather
Beyond Adventure
The Hillwalker's Manual
Outdoor Photography
The Hillwalker's Guide to
    Mountaineering
Map and Compass

MINI GUIDES
Avalanche!
Snow
Pocket First Aid and Wilderness
    Medicine
Navigation

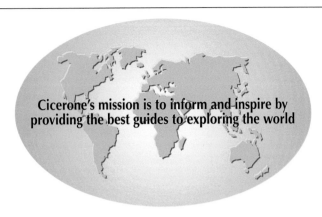

Cicerone's mission is to inform and inspire by
providing the best guides to exploring the world

Since its foundation over 30 years ago, Cicerone has specialised in
publishing guidebooks and has built a reputation for quality and reliability.
It now publishes nearly 300 guides to the major destinations for outdoor
enthusiasts, including Europe, UK and the rest of the world.

Written by leading and committed specialists, Cicerone guides are
recognised as the most authoritative. They are full of information, maps and
illustrations so that the user can plan and complete a successful and safe
trip or expedition – be it a long face climb, a walk over Lakeland fells, an
alpine traverse, a Himalayan trek or a ramble in the countryside.

With a thorough introduction to assist planning, clear diagrams, maps and
colour photographs to illustrate the terrain and route, and accurate and
detailed text, Cicerone guides are designed for ease of use and access to
the information.

If the facts on the ground change, or there is any aspect of a guide that you
think we can improve, we are always delighted to hear from you.

Cicerone Press
2 Police Square Milnthorpe Cumbria LA7 7PY
Tel:01539 562 069   Fax:01539 563 417
e-mail:info@cicerone.co.uk   web:www.cicerone.co.uk